C O N T E N T

American Patchwork Quilt D

American Patchwork Quilt Designs

★Published by ONDORISHA PUBLISHERS, LTD.,11-11 Nishigoken-cho, Shinjuku-ku, Tokyo 162, Japan.
★Sole Overseas Distributor: Japan Publications Trading Co.,Ltd.
  P.O.Box 5030 Tokyo International, Tokyo, Japan.
★Distributed in the United States by Kodansha America, Inc. through Farrar, Straus & Giroux,
  19 Union Square West, New York, NY10003.
  Australia by Bookwise International, 54 Crittenden Road, Findon, South Australia 5023, Australia.
  British Isles & European Continent by Premier Book Marketing Ltd., 1 Gower Street, London WC1E 6HA

10 9 8 7 6 5 4

ISBN 0-87040-744-9
Printed in Japan

Instructions on page 2.

Small Coverlet

*Appliqué Pattern
(Rose Wreath)*

Quilting Pattern

I

Small Coverlet, *shown on page 1.*

MATERIALS: Cotton fabric for appliqué: Light pink, 90cm by 15cm(36″×6″); moss green, 90cm by 30cm (36″×12″); ivory, 90cm by 10cm (36″×4″); blue gray and peppermint green, 90cm by 5cm (36″×2″) each; scrap of floral print. Unbleached sheeting for background and binding, 90cm by 250cm (36″× 100″). Cotton fabric for backing and lining, 90cm by 240cm (36″×96″) each. Quilt batting, 120cm (48″) square. Six-strand embroidery floss, No. 25 in lavender and sage green. Pink satin ribbon, 0.9cm by 70cm(⅜″×28″).
FINISHED SIZE: 110cm(44″) square. **DIRECTIONS:** 1. Appliqué rose wreath on 4 pieces of A. (Transfer appliqué pattern onto background fabric. Make templates of rose, bud and leaf. Cut out appliqué pieces using templates.) 2. Transfer quilting pattern onto 5 pieces of B. 3. Join pieces of A and B together following diagram. 4. Pin and baste top, quilt batting and backing together. Round corners. Quilt on quilting lines of pieces of B and then all over. 5. Place quilted piece on lining and bind edges all around. Sew on ribbon bows.

※Add 1cm (⅜″) for seam allowance unless otherwise indicated.

A
Cut 4 pieces.

(14⅜″)

(14⅜″)

B
Cut 4 pieces.

36

※Place pieces of A following diagram and reversing patterns.
※ Draw diagonal lines, 1.4cm (½″) apart, in two directions and quilt on lines.

Strip for binding
※ No seam allowance

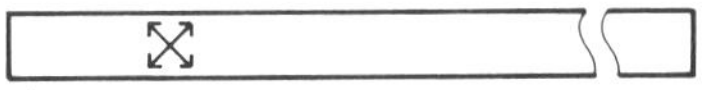

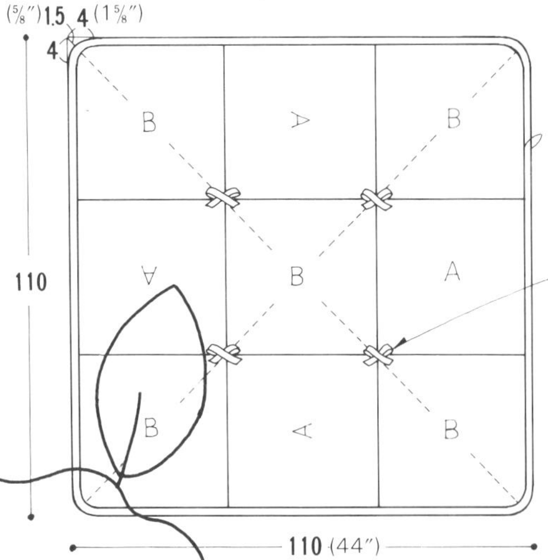

3
(1¼″)

(⅜″)1.5 4 (1⅝″)
4

450 (Join pieces.)
(180″)

110

110 (44″)

Bind edges with bias-cut strip (see page 67).

Attach ribbon bow with 3 strands of sewing thread.

How to join

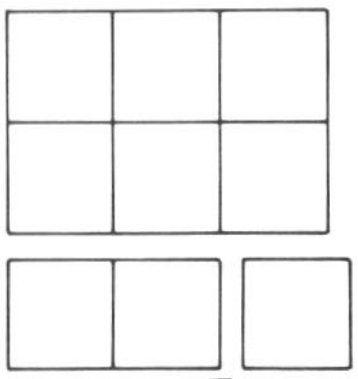

☆ Quilt batting. . . Cut into 120cm (48″) square.
Fabric for backing. . . Join two pieces at canter to make 120cm (48″) square.
Fabric for lining . . . do.

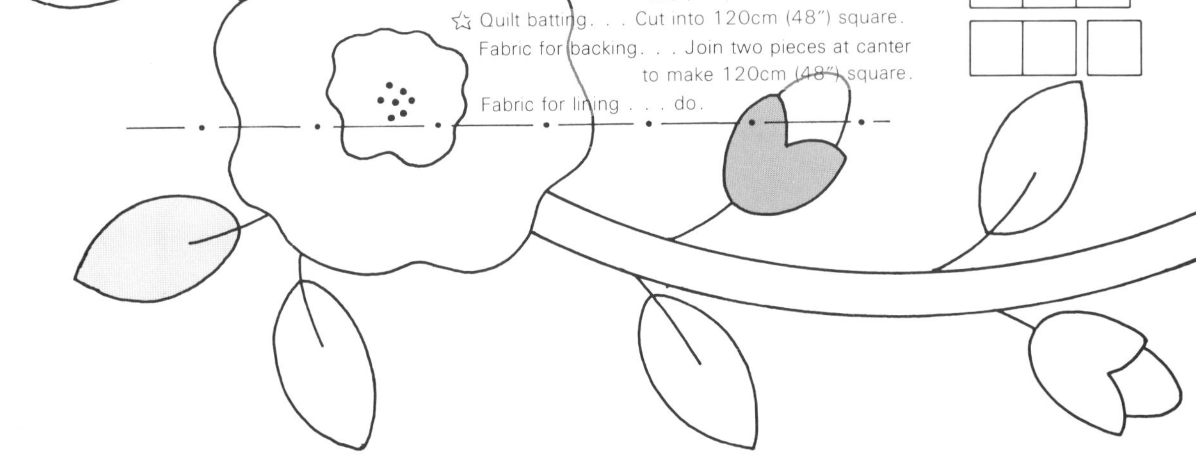

2

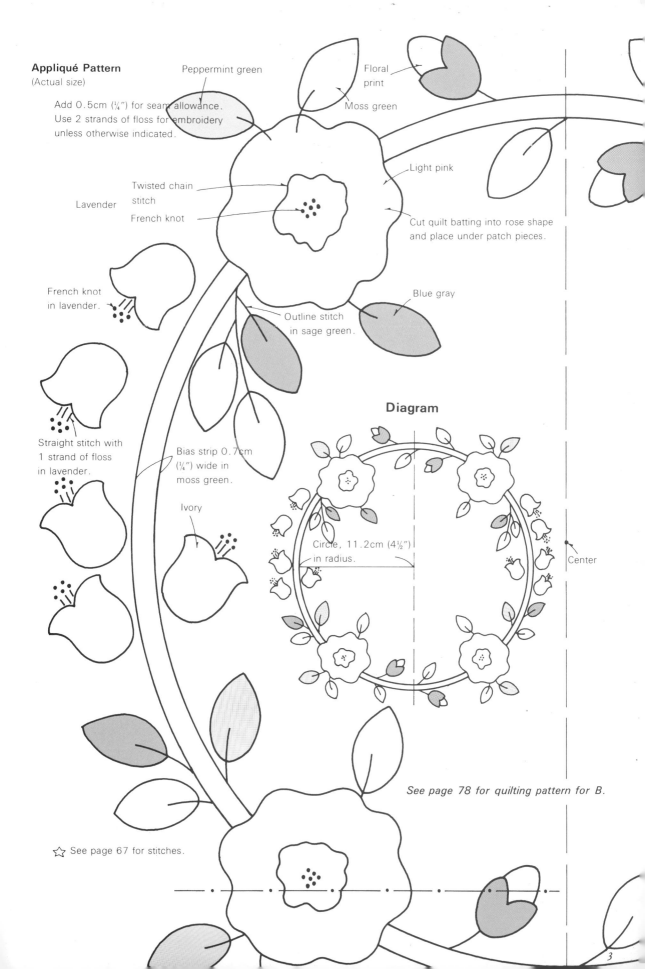

Appliqué Pattern
(Actual size)

Add 0.5cm (¼″) for seam allowance.
Use 2 strands of floss for embroidery
unless otherwise indicated.

Peppermint green

Floral print

Moss green

Twisted chain stitch

Lavender

French knot

Light pink

Cut quilt batting into rose shape
and place under patch pieces.

French knot
in lavender.

Blue gray

Outline stitch
in sage green.

Straight stitch with
1 strand of floss
in lavender.

Bias strip 0.7cm
(¼″) wide in
moss green.

Ivory

Diagram

Circle, 11.2cm (4½″)
in radius.

Center

See page 78 for quilting pattern for B.

☆ See page 67 for stitches.

Log Cabin

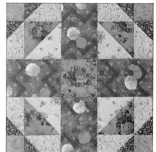

Flying Geese

Pillows

Instructions for (**A**) on page 6
and for (**B**) on page 7.

Log Cabin Pillows, *shown on pages 4 & 5.*

MATERIALS (FOR ONE PILLOW): 4 sets of 7 different prints. Cotton fabric for back, 50cm by 47cm (20" × 18¾"). Fabric for backing and quilt batting, 4 sets of 25cm (10") square each. 40cm (16") long zipper. Inner pillow stuffed with kapok, 45cm (18") square. **FIN-** **ISHED SIZE:** 45cm (18") square. **DIRECTIONS:** 1. Join pieces to make 4 sets of log cabins. 2. Join log cabins together. 3. Sew zipper onto back pieces. 4. With right sides facing, sew front and back together. Turn to right side and insert inner pillow.

Cutting Diagram
　※ Add 1cm (⅜") for seam allowance.

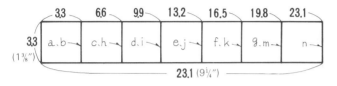

Front (Piecing Diagram)
※ Cut back pieces same size as Flying Geese pillow. 1.2cm (½") allowance for folding is included in front pieces.

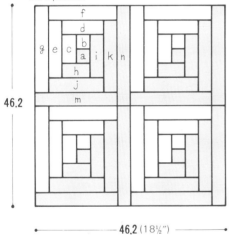

Use same color as (a) for each block.

a ············ Medium
b.c.d.e.f.g ·Light shabe
h.i.j.k.m.n ··Dark shabe

☆ Cut 4 pieces of 25cm (10") square from backing and quilt batting.

How to piece
1. Draw quilting lines on backing with pencil. Mark at 3.3cm (1⅜") intervals.

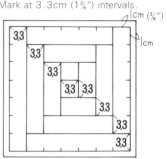

2. Pin and baste backing and batting together.

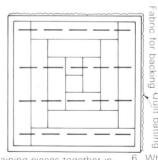

3. With right sides facing, place (a) and (b) at center of batting and pin. Sew all layers along seam line.

Quilt batting

4. Turn to right side. Place (c) on (a) and (b) with right sides facing and sew in same manner.

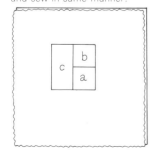

5. Sew remaining pieces together in same manner. (Check size placing pattern on joined piece.)

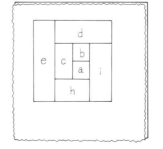

6. When joining last pieces, sew top pieces only leaving 3cm (1¼") (shown in bold lines) of backing and batting free.

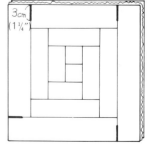

How to piece blocks

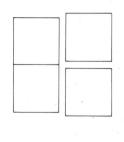

1. With right sides facing, sew 2 blocks together.
2. Cut off seam allowance of batting and place on pieced blocks. Place fabric for lining on top, turn in seam allowance and slip-stitch.

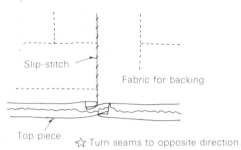

Slip-stitch

Fabric for backing

Top piece

☆ Turn seams to opposite direction.

Piecing Diagram

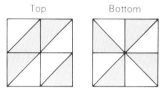

Top   Bottom

Reference

Flying Geese Pillows, *shown on pages 4 & 5.*

MATERIALS (FOR ONE) : 7 different prints: 30cm by 20cm (12″×8″) each for (a), (c) and (f); 60cm by 20cm (24″×8″) for (b) and (d) ; 40cm by 20cm (16″×8″) for (e) and (g); 80cm by 20cm (32″×8″) for (h). Fabric for lining, 50cm by 47cm (20″×18¾″). Fabric for backing and quilt batting, 47cm (18¾″) square each. 40cm (16″) long zipper. Inner pillow stuffed with kapok, 45cm (18″) square.

FINISHED SIZE: 45cm (18″) square. **DIRECTIONS:** 1. Sew patch pieces together. 2. Pin and baste pieced top, batting and backing together and quilt. 3. Sew zipper onto back pieces. 4. With right sides facing, sew front and back together. Turn to right side. Insert inner pillow.

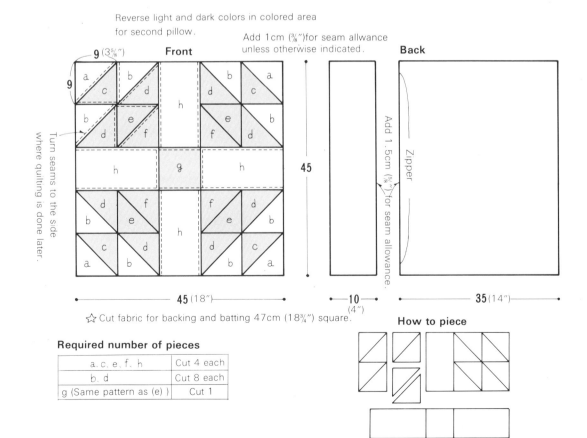

Reverse light and dark colors in colored area for second pillow.

Add 1cm (⅜″)for seam allwance unless otherwise indicated.

☆ Cut fabric for backing and batting 47cm (18¾″) square.

Turn seams to the side where quilting is done later.

Add 1.5cm (⅝″) for seam allowance.

Zipper

45

9 (3⅝″)

9

45 (18″)

10 (4″)

35 (14″)

Front   Back

How to piece

Required number of pieces

a, c, e, f, h	Cut 4 each
b, d	Cut 8 each
g (Same pattern as (e))	Cut 1

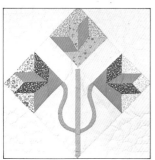

North Carolina Lily

Quilting Pattern

Small Coverlet

Instructions on page 10.

Small Coverlet, *shown on pages 8 & 9.*

MATERIALS: Fabric for patchwork: Solids and prints in blue, pink, red, yellow and sage green shades (see photo). Cotton fabric: Ivory, 90cm by 250cm(36″×100″); light blue, 35cm by 145cm (14″×58″). Fabric for lining, 90cm by 286cm (36″×114⅜″). Quilt batting, 120cm by 286cm (48″×114⅜″). **FINISHED SIZE:** 139cm (55⅝″)

square. **DIRECTIONS:** 1. Sew patch pieces together. Appliqué stems. Make 9 blocks of lilies. 2. Transfer quilting pattern onto ivory fabric. Join lily and ivory blocks together following diagram. 3. Sew borders A and B all around. 4. Pin and baste pieced top, batting and lining together and quilt. 5. Bind edges with (c).

※Add 1cm (⅜″) for seam allowance except patch pieces.
　Add 0.7cm (¼″) to patch pieces. Use prints and solids in blue shade for lilies unless otherwise indicated.

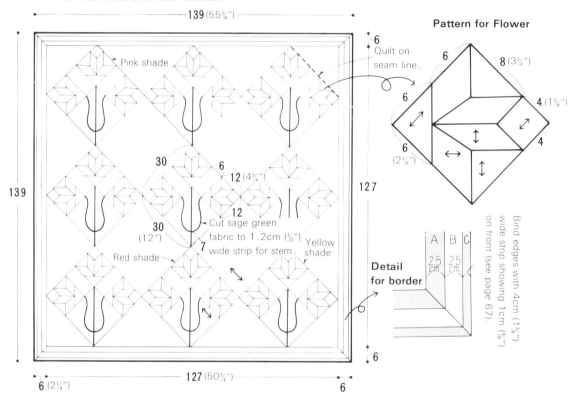

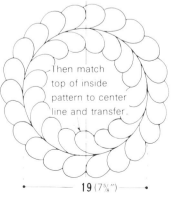

Cut 4 pieces of 4.5cm (1¾″) by 141cm (56¾″) for border from ivory fabric and then cut out patch pieces. Join 2 pieces of batting at center to make 143cm (57¼″) square. Join pieces of lining in same manner. Cut 4 pieces each.

How to piece

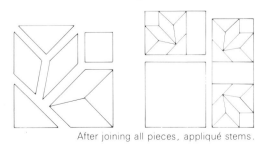

After joining all pieces, appliqué stems.

How to transfer quilting pattern

Draw 19cm (7⅝″) diameter circle. Then transfer pattern matching center of pattern and circle. For second half bring bottom part of pattern to center top and transfer pattern outside the circle.

Then match top of inside pattern to center line and transfer.

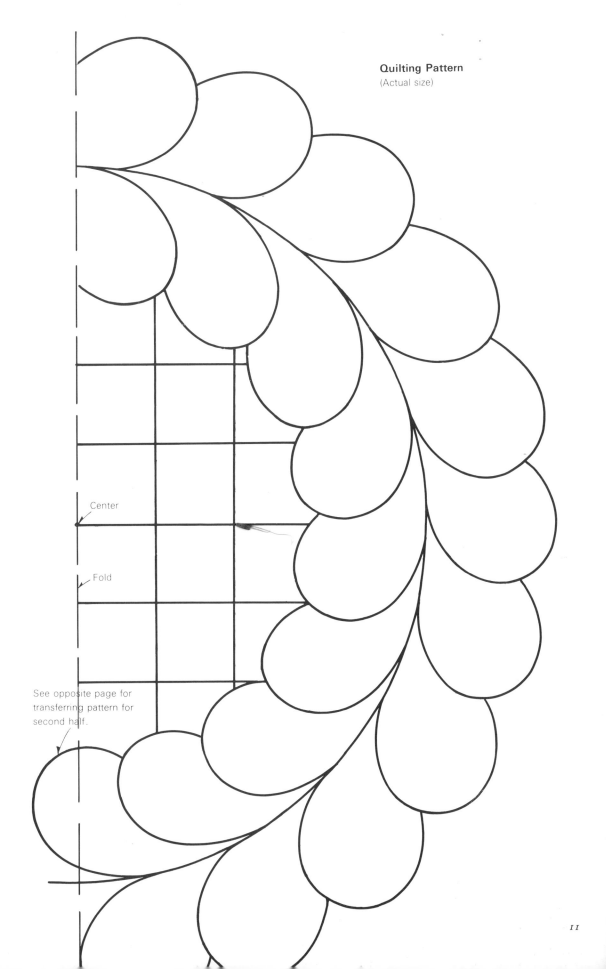

Quilting Pattern
(Actual size)

Center

Fold

See opposite page for
transferring pattern for
second half.

Star of Bethlehem

Quilting Pattern

Wall Hanging

Instructions on page 14.

Wall Hanging, *shown on pages 12 & 13.*

MATERIALS: Fabric for patchwork, border and binding (see photo for colors and designs). Fabric for lining, 90cm by 310cm (36″×124″). Quilt batting, 120cm by 310cm (48″×124″). **FINISHED SIZE:** About 150cm (60″) square. **DIRECTIONS:** 1. Join pieces for star and border following photo. 2. Join pieced star and side pieces. Join pieced square and triangles for border. 3. Join pieced center and border. 4. Pin and baste pieced top, batting and lining together and quilt. 5. Bind edges with 4cm(1⅝″) wide strip showing 1cm(⅜″) on front.

※ Add 0.7cm (¼″) all around
for seam allowance.

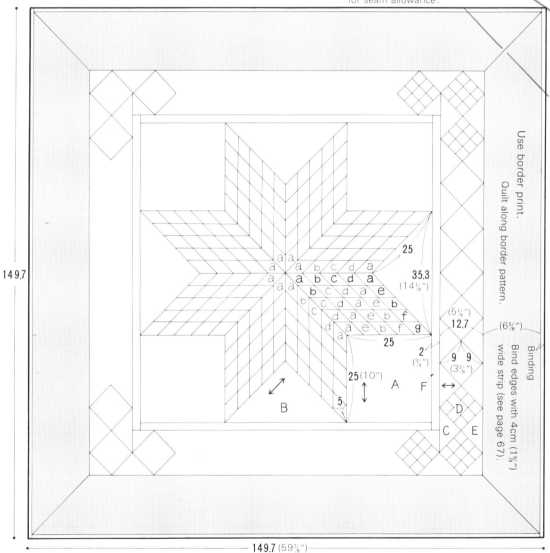

149.7

149.7 (59⅞″)

25

35.3
(14⅛″)

(5⅛″)
12.7

(6⅝″)

2
(¾″)

9 9
(3⅝″)

25

25(10″)

5

A   F

B

D

C   E

Use border print.

Quilt along border pattern.

Binding

Bind edges with 4cm (1⅝″) wide strip (see page 67).

☆ Join 2 pieces of batting at center to make 155cm (62″) square. Join pieces of lining in same manner.

How to piece

See page 35 for patterns of (a)—(g),
(C)—(F) and quilting patterns.

Quilting pattern for **Block A** (dark lines)

Fold

Fold

Quilting pattern for **Block B** (light lines)

15

Double Wedding Ring

Bedspread

Instructions on page 18.

Bedspread, *shown on pages 16 & 17.*

MATERIALS: Fabric for patches: Moss green, 90cm by 110cm (36″×44″); plum, 90cm by 140cm (36″×56″); lavender, 90cm (36″) square; ivory (including binding), 90cm by 300cm (36″×120″); print with large design for center of each circle, 48 pieces. Fabric for lining and backing, 90cm by 430cm (36″×172″) each. Quilt batting, 120cm by 340cm (48″×136″). **FINISHED SIZE:** 208.5cm by 166cm (83⅜″×66⅜″). **DIRECTIONS:** 1. Join pieces for rings as shown on page 39. 2. Join pieces for border. Pin batting, backing and border together. Place pieced rings on top and baste. 3. Turn in outer edges of rings and slip-stitch to border. 4. Quilt along seams of rings. 5. Draw diagonal lines, 3cm (1¼″) apart, on border and quilt along lines. 6. Place quilted top on lining and bind edges mitering corners.

Required number of pieces

a	Moss green	Cut 220
b	Moss green	Cut 28
	Lavender	Cut 192
c	Moss green	Cut 56
	Plum	Cut 384
d	Moss green	Cut 28
	Lavender	Cut 192
e	Ivory	Cut 110
f	Print fabric	Cut 48

Patterns
(Actual size)

※ Add 0.7cm(¼″) seam allowance.

See page 39 for joining.

Quilt inside of seams for pieces placed on outer edges.

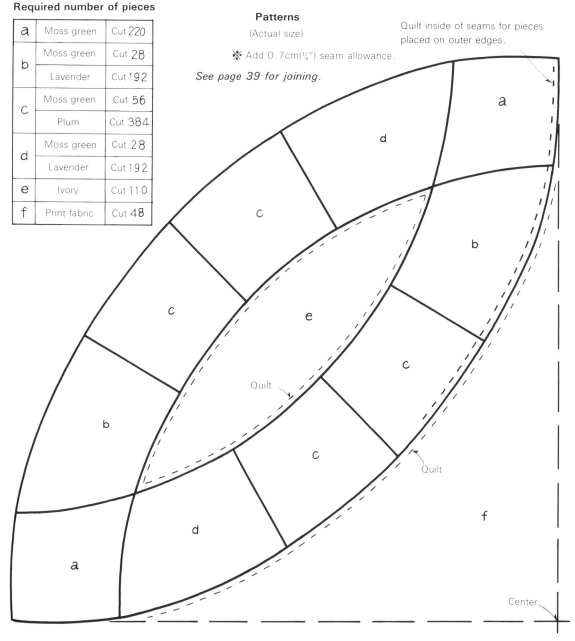

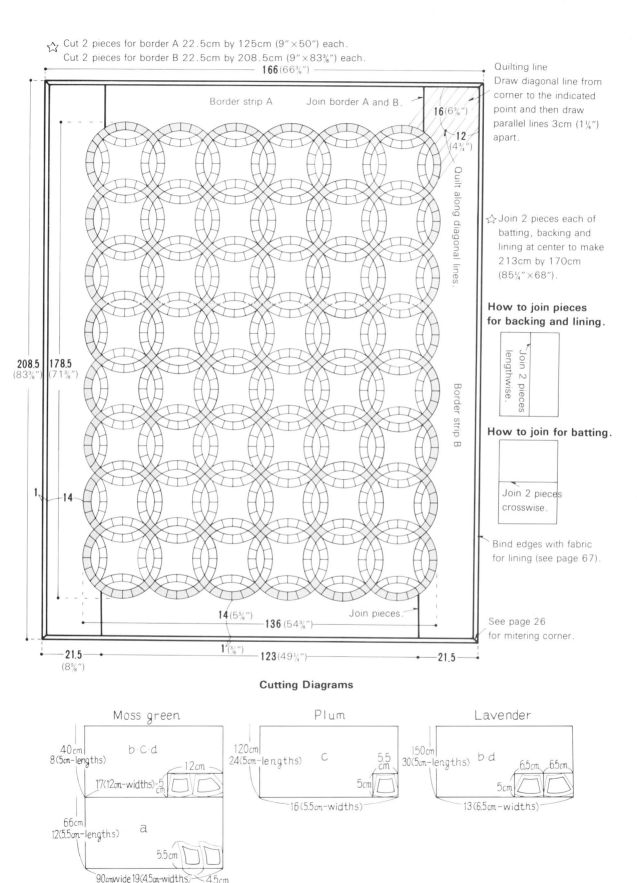

☆ Cut 2 pieces for border A 22.5cm by 125cm (9″×50″) each.
   Cut 2 pieces for border B 22.5cm by 208.5cm (9″×83⅜″) each.

166 (66⅜″)

Border strip A   Join border A and B.

Quilting line
Draw diagonal line from
corner to the indicated
point and then draw
parallel lines 3cm (1¼″)
apart.

16 (6⅜″)

12 (4¾″)

Quilt along diagonal lines.

☆ Join 2 pieces each of
batting, backing and
lining at center to make
213cm by 170cm
(85¼″×68″).

**How to join pieces
for backing and lining.**

Join 2 pieces
lengthwise.

Border strip B

208.5 (83⅜″)   178.5 (71⅜″)

How to join for batting.

Join 2 pieces
crosswise.

Bind edges with fabric
for lining (see page 67).

1

14

14 (5⅝″)   Join pieces.
136 (54⅜″)

See page 26
for mitering corner.

1 (⅜″)
123 (49¼″)

21.5 (8⅝″)   21.5

Cutting Diagrams

Moss green

40cm
8 (5cm-lengths)   b·c·d   12cm

17 (12cm-widths)—5 cm

66cm
12 (5.5cm-lengths)   a

5.5 cm

90cm wide 19 (4.5cm-widths)   4.5cm

Plum

120cm
24 (5cm-lengths)   c   5.5 cm

5cm

16 (5.5cm-widths)

Lavender

150cm
30 (5cm-lengths)   b·d   6.5cm   6.5cm

5cm

13 (6.5cm-widths)

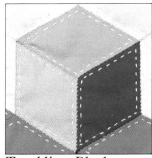

Tumbling Blocks

Nine Patch

Pillows
and Mat

Instructions for
Pillows on page 22
and for Mat on page 23.

Pillows, *shown on pages 20 & 21.*

MATERIALS: (FOR ONE): Fabric for patches (a), (g), (b) and (c), 90cm by 5cm (36″×2″) each; for (d), (e), (h) and (f), 70cm by 5cm (28″×2″) each. Unbleached cotton fabric (including pieces (i)—(o), 90cm by 40cm(36″×16″). Fabric for binding (same as (d)), 50cm (20″) square. Flannel for backing, 45cm by 36cm (18″×14⅜″). 40cm (16″) long zipper. Six-strand embroidery floss, No. 25 in white. Kapok, 400g. Fabric for inner pillow, 90cm by 40cm (36″×16″). **FINISHED SIZE:** 44.4cm by 36cm (17¾″×14⅜″) **DIRECTIONS:** 1. Join pieces and join to border. 2. Pin and baste pieced top and flannel and quilt. 3. Sew zipper onto back pieces. 4. With wrong sides of front and back facing, bind edges all around. 5. Make inner pillow, 43cm by 34cm (17¼″×13⅝″) and stuff with kapok.

Patterns
(Actual size)

※ Add 0.7cm(¼″) for seam allowance.

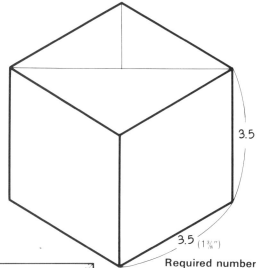

3.5

3.5 (1⅜″)

※ Add 1cm (⅜″) for seam allowance unless otherwise indicated.

Front

36.4 (14½″)

Quilt with 2 strands of embroidery floss.

34 (13⅝″)

28 (11¼″)

3 (1¼″)

42.4 (17″)

3　Border strip　Unbleached

Required number of pieces

a	Cut14	h	Cut1
b	14	i	4
c	13	j	2
d	11	k	1
e	10	m	10
f	10	n	2
g	1	o	2

Use same fabric for (a) and (g). Use same fabric for (e) and (h). Use same fabric for (i),(j),(k),(m),(n) and (o).

How to piece

Back

Unbleached
Cut 2.

Zipper

17 (6¾″)

42.4

Add 3cm (1¼″) for seam allowance for sewing zipper.

Strip for binding.　No seam allowance

3.5

(1⅜″)

170 (Join pieces.)
(68″)

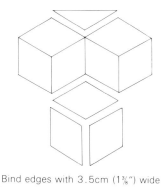

Bind edges with 3.5cm (1⅜″) wide strip showing 1cm on front (see page 67).

Mat, *shown on pages 20 & 21.*

MATERIALS: Fabric for patches: 90cm by 30cm (36″× 12″) for (a); 90cm by 36cm (36″×14⅜″) for (b); 90cm by 45cm (36″×18″) for (c); 90cm by 60cm (36″×24″) for (d) and (e); 34cm (13⅜″) square for (f). Fabric for border and binding, 92cm by 72cm (36¾″×28¾″). Fabric for lining, 94cm by 128cm (37⅝″×51¼″). Quilt batting, 94cm by 260cm (37⅝″×104″). **FINISHED SIZE:** 125.5cm by 91.5cm (50¼″×36⅝″). **DIRECTIONS:** 1. Join pieces from (a) to (f) and borders (A) and (B). 2. Pin and baste pieced top, batting and lining together and quilt. 3. Bind edges with 7cm wide strip showing 3.5cm (1⅜″) on front.

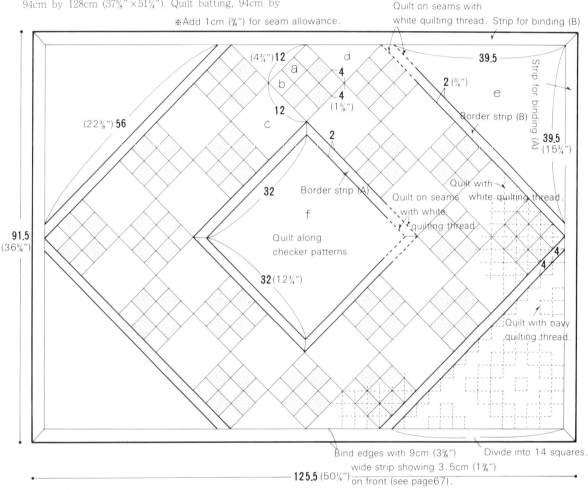

※Add 1cm (⅜″) for seam allowance.

☆ Cut 2 pieces of 94cm by 128cm (37⅝″×51¼″) from batting.
Cut 94cm by 128cm (37⅝″×51¼″) from fabric for lining.

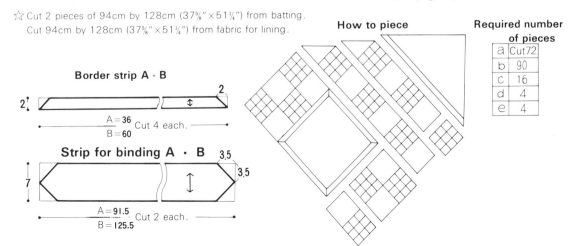

Border strip A · B

2

2

A=36
B=60 Cut 4 each.

Strip for binding A · B

3.5

3.5

7

A=91.5
B=125.5 Cut 2 each.

How to piece

Required number of pieces		
a	Cut72	
b	90	
c	16	
d	4	
e	4	

Nine Patch

Bedspread

Instructions on page 26.

Bedspread, *shown on pages 24 & 25.*

MATERIALS: Fabric for patches: Prints, 85 pieces of 13cm (5¼″) square each; black, 90cm by 195cm(36″×78″) for 86 pieces. Pink sheeting, 90cm by 330cm (36″×132″). Blue sheeting for lining, 90cm by 910cm (36″×364″). Quilt batting, 120cm by 550cm (48″×220″). Pink yarn. **FINISHED SIZE:** 189cm by 269cm (75⅝″×107⅝″).

DIRECTIONS: 1. Join pieces together and join to borders A and B. 2. Pin and baste pieced top, batting and lining together and quilt. 3. Turn excess lining on top, turn in seam allowance and slip-stitch. Tuft with pink yarn.

※ Add 1cm (⅜″) for seam allowance.

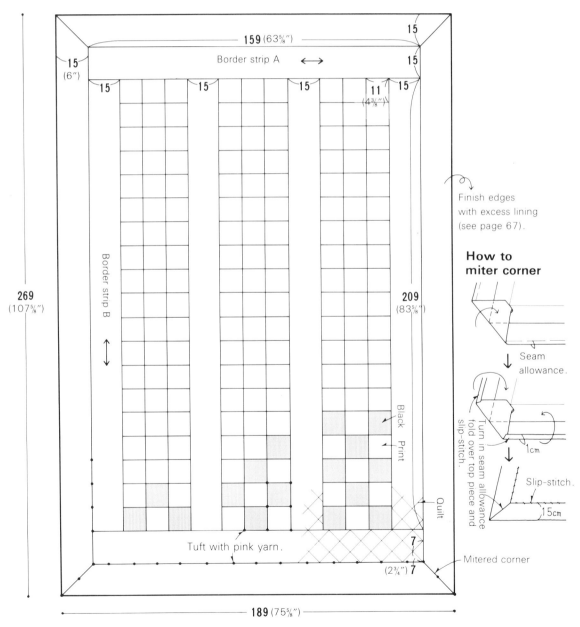

Join 2 pieces of batting at center to make 191cm by 271cm (76⅜″×108⅜″).
Join 3 pieces of lining to make 221cm by 301cm (88⅜″×120⅜″).

Potholders, *shown on page 40.*

MATERIALS: Scraps for patch pieces. Quilt batting and fabric for lining, 20cm (8") square each. Fabric for binding and hanging loop. **FINISHED SIZE:** 20cm (8") square. **DIRECTIONS:** 1. Join pieces following diagram.

2. Pin and baste pieced top, batting and lining together and quilt. 3. Bind edges with bias-cut strip and attach loop for hanging.

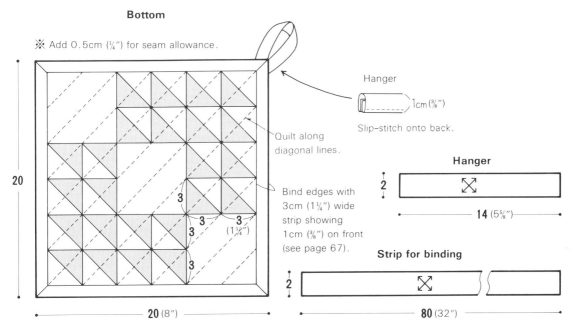

Bottom

※ Add 0.5cm (¼") for seam allowance.

Quilt along diagonal lines.

Bind edges with 3cm (1¼") wide strip showing 1cm (⅜") on front (see page 67).

20

3
3   3
3   (1¼")
3

3

20 (8")

Hanger

1cm (⅜")

Slip-stitch onto back.

Hanger

2

14 (5⅝")

Strip for binding

2

80 (32")

☆ Cut out 20cm (8") square each from fabric for lining and batting.

Top

Quilt.

Start joining at center
and work outward following diagram.

Center

0.5cm (¼")

Quilt.

Lightest color

Darkest color

Join pieces as shown placing lightest
color at right top and darkest color
at left bottom.

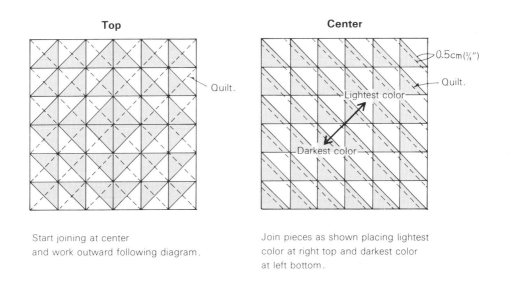

(**Make two more potholders.**)

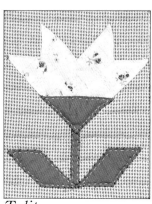

Tulip

Table Mats
and Napkins

Instructions on page 30.

Table Mats & Napkins, *shown on pages 28 & 29.*

For Table Mats MATERIALS: (FOR ONE): Scraps for appliqué and patch pieces. Fabric for lining and flannel, 30cm (12″) square each. Binding tape, 1.5cm by 135cm (⅝″×54″) including 10cm (4″) for loops for buttons. 8 buttons, 1.5cm (⅝″) in diameter. **FINISHED SIZE:** 30cm (12″) square. **DIRECTIONS:** 1. Join 3 pieces for tulip mat and nine squares for nine-patch mat. 2. Appliqué tulips in place. 3. Pin and baste top, flannel

and lining together and quilt. 4. Bind edges with bias binding tape. You can use mats individually or make a big one by connecting loops and buttons. **For Napkins MATERIALS:** (FOR ONE): Scraps for appliqué pieces. Fabric for background, 43cm (17¼″) square. **FINISHED SIZE:** 40cm (16″) square. **DIRECTIONS:** 1. Make hem all around to make 40cm (16″) square. 2. Appliqué tulip in place.

Table mats

※ Add 0.7cm (¼″) for seam allowance.

Attach loops or buttons when joining more than two mats.

Tulip's mat — Loop for button

10 (4″) 10 10

30

Quilt horizontally 1.5cm (⅝″) apart.

30 (12″)

☆ Cut out 30cm (12″) square each from fabric for lining and flannel.

Nine-patch mat

10 10 10

Quilt.

Place for button
Bind edges with 2.8cm (1⅛″) wide strip showing 0.7cm (¼″) on front (see page 67).

0.7

30

How to attach loop for button

Back

0.5cm

0.7cm

Fold 5cm (2″) long binding tape in half lengthwise, turn in seam allowance and stitch. Fold in half as shown, insert ends into binding and stitch.

Appliqué Patterns for Mat and Napkin (Actual size)

Add 0.5cm (¼″) for seam allowance.

Flower

Leaf

Stem

Calyx

Quilt.

Required number of pieces

	Table mat	Napkin
Flower	Cut 8.	Cut 4.
Leaf	4	2
Calyx	2	1
Stem	2	1

Napkin

Place for appliqué.

8cm (3¼″)

Center

1cm (⅜″)

30

Scissors' Case, *shown on page 44.*

MATERIALS: Pink sheeting, fabric for lining and quilt batting, 25cm by 35cm (10″×14″) each. Fabric for binding, 40cm by 30cm (16″×12″). One button, 1.5cm (⅝″) in diameter. **FINISHED SIZE:** See diagram. **DIRECTIONS:** 1. Pin and baste sheeting, batting and lining together and quilt. Make front in same manner but quilt on tulip design. 2. Bind top edges of front with bias-cut strip. 3. With wrong sides of front and back facing, bind edges all around catching ends of loop at top.

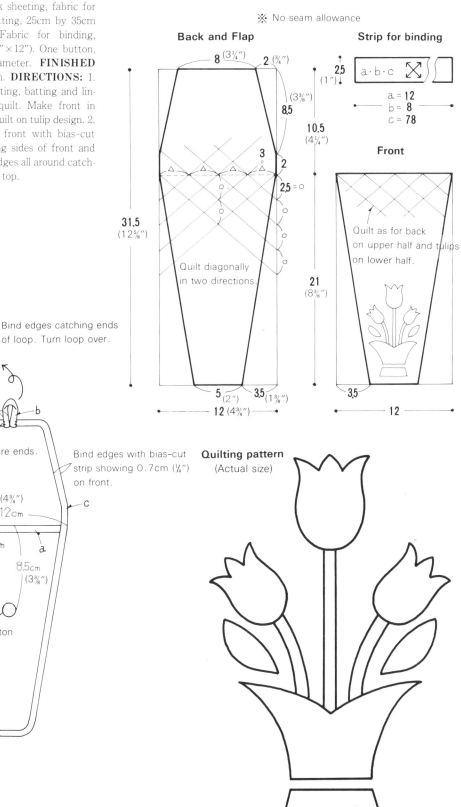

※ No seam allowance

Back and Flap

8 (3¼″) 2 (¾″)

(3⅜″)

8.5

10.5 (4¼″)

2.5 (1″)

3

2

2.5 = ○

Quilt diagonally in two directions.

31.5 (12⅝″)

5 (2″) 3.5 (1⅜″)

12 (4¾″)

Strip for binding

2.5 (1″)

a·b·c

a = 12
b = 8
c = 78

Front

Quilt as for back on upper half and tulips on lower half.

21 (8⅜″)

3.5

12

Bind edges catching ends of loop. Turn loop over.

0.7cm

b

Secure ends.

Bind edges with bias-cut strip showing 0.7cm (¼″) on front.

c

(4¾″)
12cm

0.7cm (¼″)

a

8.5cm (3⅜″)

31.5cm (12⅝″)

Button

Quilting pattern (Actual size)

31

Variation of Drunkard's Path

Tablecloth

Instructions on page 34.

Tablecloth, *shown on pages 32 & 33.*

MATERIALS: Different prints in dark, medium and light shades for patches (see list on next page for required number of pieces). Fabric for borders (medium shade), 64cm by 124cm (25⅝″ × 49⅝″). Fabric for corners, 64cm by 8cm(25⅝″ × 3¼″). Fabric for lining, 90cm by 252cm (36″ × 100¾″). Quilt batting, 120cm by 274cm (48″ × 109⅝″). **FINISHED SIZE:** About 134cm (53⅝″) square. **DIRECTIONS:** 1. Join fan shape and the rest to make square. Join squares starting at center. 2. Join borders and corner blocks with pieced squares. 3. Pin and baste top, batting and lining together and quilt along seams of each square. 4. With right sides facing, sew border of lining along edges. 5. Turn in seam allowance and slip-stitch onto lining. 6. Quilt along quilting lines on borders and corner blocks.

※Add 0.7cm (¼″) for seam allowance to pieces (a) to (h). Add 1cm for seam allowance to corner blocks and borders.

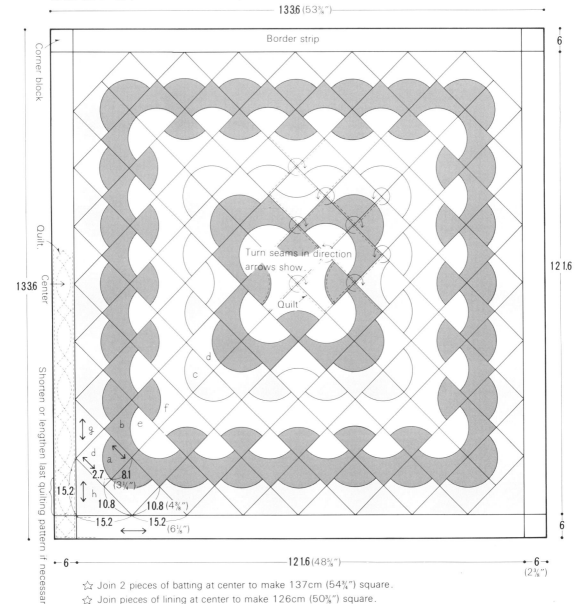

☆ Join 2 pieces of batting at center to make 137cm (54¾″) square.
☆ Join pieces of lining at center to make 126cm (50⅜″) square.

Required number of pieces

Dark shade		Medium shade				Light shade		Corner blocks		Borders	
a	b	c	d	g	h	e	f	Right side	Wrong side	Right side	Wrong side
Cut 60.	32 "	16 "	40 "	24 "	4 "	36 "	40 "	4	4	4	4

Prepare required number of pieces in dark, medium and light shades.

How to join

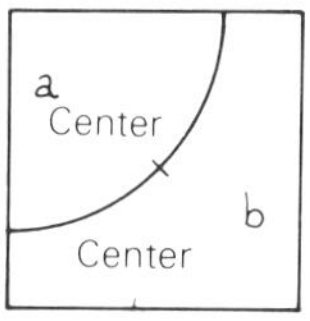

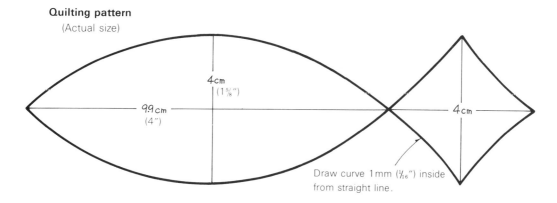

a Center

b

Center

1. Mark at corner of each piece. With right sides facing, pin 2 pieces together matching marks. Then pin at each side. Pin between center and side at 1cm intervals. Stitch along curve and take a backstitch at center.
2. Make squares in this way and join them starting at center.

Quilting pattern
(Actual size)

4cm
(1⅝")

9.9cm
(4")

4cm

Draw curve 1mm (¹⁄₁₆") inside from straight line.

Continued from page 14.

Patterns

a~g

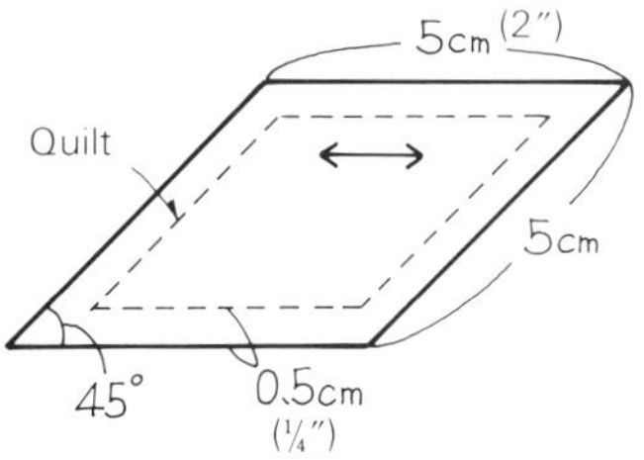

5cm (2")

Quilt

5cm

45° 0.5cm (¼")

C~F

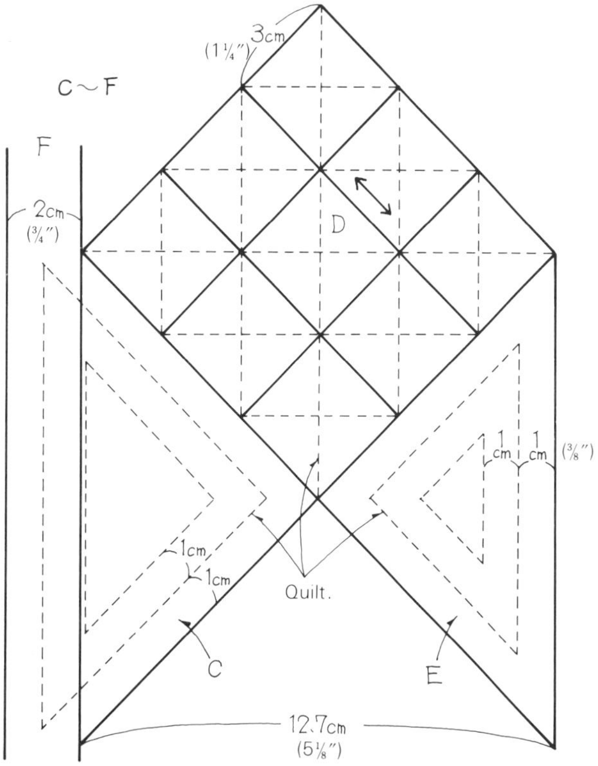

F

3cm (1¼")

2cm (¾")

D

1 cm 1 cm 1 (⅜")

1cm
1cm

Quilt.

C

E

12.7cm (5⅛")

Ohio Star

Nine Patch

Tray Mat
and Coasters

Instructions for
Tray Mat on page 38
and for Coasters on page 39.

Tray Mat, *shown on pages 36 & 37.*

MATERIALS: Fabric for patches: Scraps for (a), (b) and (c); 50cm by 20cm (20″×8″) for (d), (e) and (f). Fabric for lining, 42cm by 28cm (16¾″×11¼″). Quilt batting and backing, 39cm by 25cm (15⅝″×10″) each. Six-strand embroidery floss, No. 25 in white and navy. **FINISHED SIZE:** 39cm by 25cm (15⅝″×10″). **DIRECTIONS:** 1.

Join pieces from (a) to (f) following diagram. Appliqué and embroider on piece (d). 2. Pin and baste top, batting and backing together and quilt. 3. Pin and baste quilted piece and lining together, turn excess of lining on top and slip-stitch.

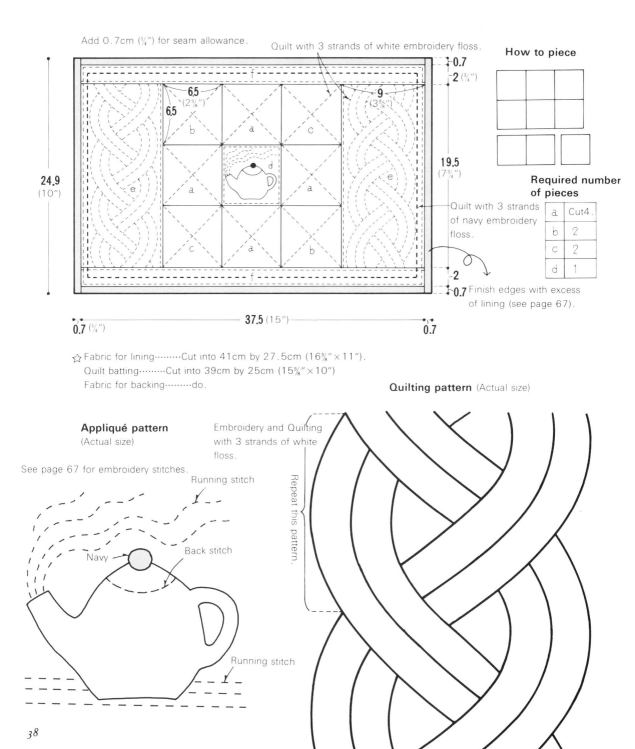

Add 0.7cm (¼″) for seam allowance.

Quilt with 3 strands of white embroidery floss.

f

0.7

2 (¾″)

6.5 (2⅝″)

6.5

9 (3⅝″)

b   a   c

d

e   a   a   e

19.5 (7¾″)

Quilt with 3 strands of navy embroidery floss.

c   a   b

f

2

24.9 (10″)

0.7

Finish edges with excess of lining (see page 67).

37.5 (15″)

0.7 (¼″)   0.7

How to piece

Required number of pieces

a	Cut 4.
b	2
c	2
d	1

☆ Fabric for lining·········Cut into 41cm by 27.5cm (16¾″×11″).
  Quilt batting·········Cut into 39cm by 25cm (15⅝″×10″)
  Fabric for backing·········do.

Appliqué pattern (Actual size)

See page 67 for embroidery stitches.

Running stitch

Navy

Back stitch

Running stitch

Embroidery and Quilting with 3 strands of white floss.

Repeat this pattern.

Quilting pattern (Actual size)

Coasters, *shown on pages 36 & 37.*

MATERIALS: (FOR ONE): Scraps of 5 different prints for patches. Fabric for lining (same as (d), 16cm (6⅜″) square. Fabric for backing and quilt batting, 13.5cm(5¾″) square each. Six-strand embroidery floss, No. 25 in white. **FINISHED SIZE:** 13.4cm (5⅜″) square. **DIREC-**

TIONS: 1. Sew pieces together to make top. 2. Pin and baste backing. batting and top together and quilt. 3. Center quilted piece on lining, fold excess lining onto top, turn in edges and slip-stitch to top.

※ Add 0.7cm (¼″) for seam allowance.

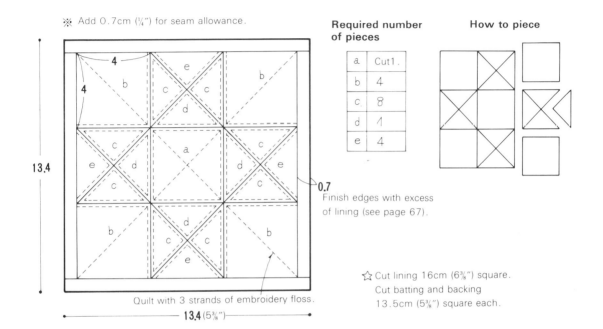

Required number of pieces

a	Cut1.
b	4
c	8
d	1
e	4

How to piece

13.4

0.7
Finish edges with excess of lining (see page 67).

Quilt with 3 strands of embroidery floss.

13.4 (5⅜″)

☆ Cut lining 16cm (6⅜″) square.
Cut batting and backing
13.5cm (5¾″) square each.

Continued from page 19.

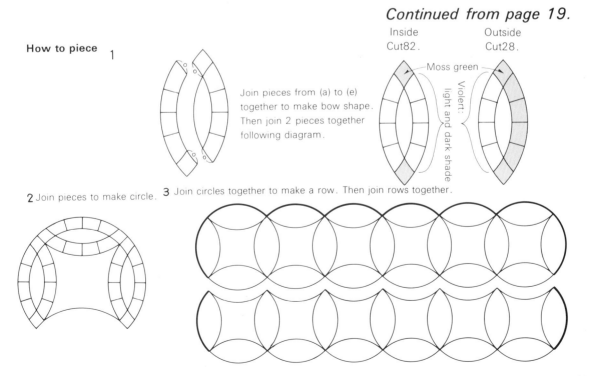

Inside
Cut82.

Outside
Cut28.

How to piece 1

Join pieces from (a) to (e) together to make bow shape. Then join 2 pieces together following diagram.

Moss green

Violet:
light and dark shade

2 Join pieces to make circle. 3 Join circles together to make a row. Then join rows together.

Instructions for Potholders on page 27 and for Mitten on page 68.

Potholders and Mitten

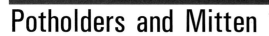

Ocean Wave

Pineapple

Instructions on pages 42 & 43.

Maple Leaf

Placemats
and Tea Cozy

Tea Cozy, *shown on page 41.*

MATERIALS: Red print, 90cm by 70cm (36″×28″). Checks (white with black grid), 92cm by 40cm (36¾″×16″). Checks (black with white grid), 50cm by 30cm (20″×12″). Gray print, 40cm by 20cm (16″×8″). Scrap of black print. Flannel, 100cm by 40cm (40″×16″). Polyester fiberfill, 90cm by 40cm (36″×16″). Six-strand embroidery floss, No. 25 in light gray. **FINISHED SIZE:**

See diagram. **DIRECTIONS:** 1. Join center and strips together to make top. Make 2 pieces for front and back. Join pieces for maples and appliqué onto front and back. 2. Pin and baste flannel and pieced top. Quilt along seams. 3. Fold 4cm (1⅝″) of bottom to wrong side, place lining along edges overlapping 1cm (⅜″) and slip-stitch. 4. Place polyester fiberfill between lining and flannel and quilt on seams. 5. With wrong sides facing, bind edges with bias-cut strip making 1.5cm (⅝″) wide on front and back and catching loop.

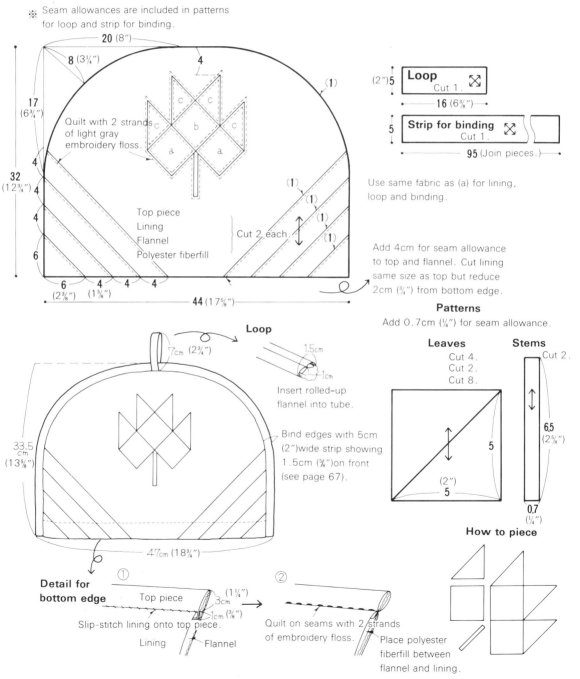

※ Seam allowances are included in patterns for loop and strip for binding.

20 (8″)
8 (3¼″)
4
17 (6¾″)
Quilt with 2 strands of light gray embroidery floss.
c c
c b c
a a
32 (12¾″)
4
4
4
6
6
4 4 4
(2⅜″) (1⅝″)
44 (17⅝″)
(1)
(1)
(1)
(1)
(1)
Top piece
Lining
Flannel
Polyester fiberfill
Cut 2 each.

(2″)5 **Loop** Cut 1.
16 (6⅜″)
5 **Strip for binding** Cut 1.
95 (Join pieces.)

Use same fabric as (a) for lining, loop and binding.

Add 4cm for seam allowance to top and flannel. Cut lining same size as top but reduce 2cm (¾″) from bottom edge.

Patterns
Add 0.7cm (¼″) for seam allowance.

Loop
7cm (2¾″)
1.5cm
1cm
Insert rolled-up flannel into tube.

Bind edges with 5cm (2″)wide strip showing 1.5cm (⅝″)on front (see page 67).

Leaves
Cut 4.
Cut 2.
Cut 8.
5
(2″)
5

Stems
Cut 2.
6,5 (2⅝″)
0,7 (¼″)

33.5 cm (13⅝″)
47cm (18¾″)

How to piece

Detail for bottom edge
① Top piece
3cm (1¼″)
1cm (⅜″)
Slip-stitch lining onto top piece.
Lining   Flannel

② Quilt on seams with 2 strands of embroidery floss. Place polyester fiberfill between flannel and lining.

Placemats, *shown on page 41.*

MATERIALS: (FOR ONE): Make second placemat reversing colors shown in parentheses. Use same color for maple leaves. Gray print, 30cm by 20cm (12″×8″). Scraps of black with white grid (white with black grid). Red print (black print), 70cm by 30cm (28″×12″). Black print (red print), 60cm by 30cm (24″×12″). Fabric for lining and flannel, 50cm by 40cm (20″×16″) each. Six -strand embroidery floss, No. 25 in gray. **FINISHED**

SIZE: 44cm by 32cm (17⅝″×12¾″).**DIRECTIONS:** 1. Join pieces (A) and (B) together. Join pieces for maples. Appliqué maples in place. 2. Pin and baste flannel and pieced top. Quilt along seams. 3. With wrong sides facing, sew quilted top and lining together leaving opening for turning. Turn to right side. Slip-stitch opening closed.

❅Add 1cm (⅜″) for seam allowance except patch pieces.

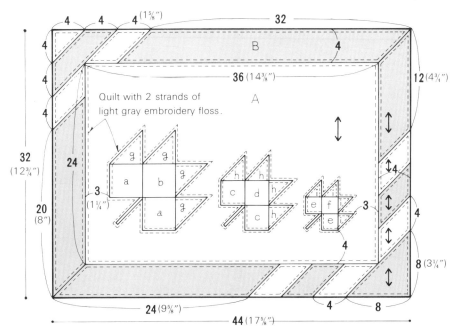

☆ Cut 46cm by 34cm (18⅜″×13⅝″) from fabric for lining.
Cut 44cm by 32vm (17⅝″×12¾″) from flannel.

Patterns

Add 0.4cm (⅛″) for seam allowance to piece of stem.
Add 0.7cm (¼″) for seam allowance to patch pieces except stem.

Leaves

a、b、c、d、e、f

g、h、i

Stems

Large ・Medium・Small
Cut 1 each.

5,5 (2¼″)
3,5 (1⅜″)
2,2 (⅞″)
0,4 (⅛″)

Leaves dimensions
4 (1⅝″)
3 (1¼″)
2 (¾″)
4
3
2

3
2
4

Required number of pieces

a	Cut 2.
b	1
c	2
d	1
e	2
f	1
g	4
h	4
i	4

B

School House ——— **A**

Bow Tie ——— **B**

Flower Basket

Six-pointed Star ——— **C**

Quilting Pattern

Pincushions, Scissors' Case and Picture

Instructions for
(A) and (B) on page 46,
for (C) and Picture on page 47,
and for Scissors' Case on page 31.

Pincushions, *shown on pages 44 & 45.*

For A: MATERIALS: Scraps for patches and for lining. Fabric for ruffle, 50cm (20″) square. Polyester fiberfill. **FINISHED SIZE:** See diagram. **DIRECTIONS:** 1. Join pieces for front. 2. Fold ruffle in half lengthwise and gather. With right sides facing, sew front and back together with gathered ruffle in between leaving opening for turning. Turn to right side, stuff with fiberfill and slip-stitch opening closed.

Border strip No seam allowance.

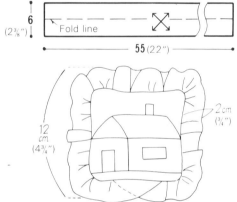

6 (2⅜″)

Fold line

55 (22″)

12 cm (4¾″)

2 cm (¾″)

Patterns (Actual size)

※ Add 0.5cm (¼″) for seam allowance.

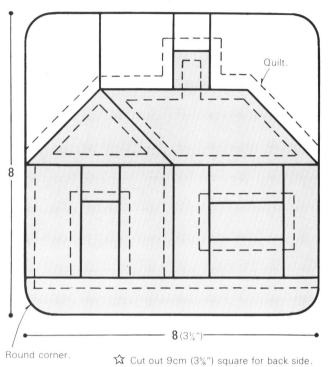

Quilt.

8

8 (3¼″)

Round corner.

☆ Cut out 9cm (3⅝″) square for back side.

FOR B: MATERIALS: Scraps for patches and for lining. Bias tape, 1.5cm (⅝″) wide. Polyester fiberfill. **FINISHED SIZE:** 10cm (4″) square. **DIRECTIONS:** 1. Join pieces for front. 2. With wrong sides of front and back facing, bind edges all around but insert fiberfill before closing completely.

How to piece

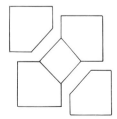

☆ Turn seams to bow side.

※ Add 0.5cm (¼″) for seam allowance.

10 (4″)

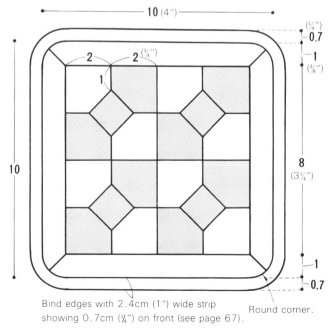

(¼″)
0.7

1 (⅜″)

2   2 (¾″)

1

10

8 (3¼″)

1

0.7

Bind edges with 2.4cm (1″) wide strip showing 0.7cm (¼″) on front (see page 67).

Round corner.

☆ Cut out 11cm (4⅜″) square for back side.

46

FOR C: MATERIALS: Scraps for patches and for lining. Polyester fiberfill. **FINISHED SIZE:** See diagram. **DIRECTIONS:** 1. Join 12 pieces of (a) together to make big hexagon. 2. With right sides facing, sew 2 pieces of (b) together. Turn to right side and stuff thinly. 3. With right sides facing and pieces (b) in between, sew front and back together leaving opening for turning.

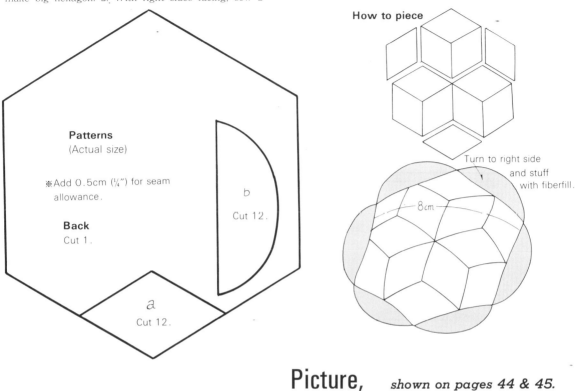

Patterns (Actual size)

✳Add 0.5cm (¼″) for seam allowance.

Back Cut 1.

b Cut 12.

a Cut 12.

How to piece

Turn to right side and stuff with fiberfill.

8cm

Picture, *shown on pages 44 & 45.*

MATERIALS: Fabric for patches: 25cm by 20cm (10″×8″) for (a); 25cm by 5cm (10″×2″) for (b); 35cm by 5cm (14″×2″) for (c) and (d). Scraps of 5 different prints. Backing and quilt batting, 50cm (20″) square each (adjust size depending on size of frame). **FINISHED SIZE:** 33.8cm by 41.3cm (13½″×16½″) (inside measurement). **DIRECTIONS:** 1. Make pattern of handle, 22cm (8¾″) wide and 17.5cm (7″) high. Cut out handle using pattern and appliqué onto background fabric. 2. Join pieces to make basket and appliqué in place. 3. Appliqué flowers, centers of flowers and buds padding with batting as you sew. 4. Place appliquéd piece on batting and frame.

See page 73 for Appliqué Patterns.

Patterns

✳ Add 0.5cm (¼″) for seam allowance.

3.5

3.5

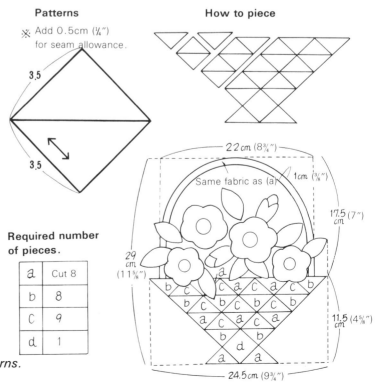

How to piece

Same fabric as (a)

22cm (8¾″)

1cm (⅜″)

17.5 (7″) cm

29 cm (11⅝″)

11.5 (4⅝″) cm

24.5cm (9¾″)

Required number of pieces.

a	Cut 8
b	8
c	9
d	1

Instructions on page 50.

Picture

Compass

Instructions on page 51.

Cosmetic Cases

Rising Star

49

Picture, *shown on page 48.*

MATERIALS: Fabric for patches: 30cm by 10cm (12″ × 4″) for (a); 30cm by 5cm (12″×2″) for (b); 40cm by 20cm (16″×8″) for (c) and (e); 30cm by 15cm (12″×6″) for (d). Fabric for background, 50cm by 60cm (20″×24″). Quilt batting, 50cm (20″) square (adjust size depending on size of frame). **FINISHED SIZE:** 33.8cm by 41.3cm (13½″ × 16½″) (inside measurement). **DIRECTIONS:** 1. Join pieces for background and star together following diagram. 2. Pin and baste pieced top and batting. Quilt diagonally in two directions on background fabric and along seams of star pieces.

How to draw quilting lines on background

Draw diagonal line from one corner to opposite corner. Draw parallel lines to this line 1.4cm (½″) apart. Draw lines in opposite direction in same manner.
(Quilt along lines except star.)

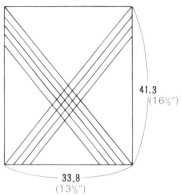

41.3 (16½″)

33.8 (13½″)

Frame

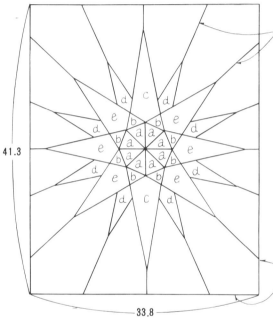

41.3

33.8

1. Place ruler connecting center and point of star. Extend line from point to edge.
2. Cut out pieces for background adding 0.7cm (¼″) for seam allowance.

Add 5cm (2″) for margin to outer edges.

How to draw

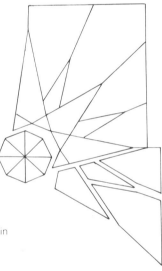

Patterns (Actual size)

※ Add 0.7cm (¼″) for seam allowance.

Quilt along border design for pieces (a).

a

b

Quilt.

d

e

c

Required number of pieces

a (Border designs)	Cut 8
b	8
c	2
d	8
e (Same as (c))	6

Cosmetic Case, *shown on page 49, top.*

MATERIALS: Scraps of 5 different prints. Fabric for lining and backing, 50cm by 17cm (20″×6¾″) each. Quilt batting, 50cm by 18cm (20″×7¼″). 20cm long zipper. **FINISHED SIZE:** See diagram. **DIRECTIONS:** 1. Join pieces to make front and back. 2. Pin and baste pieced top, batting and lining together and quilt along seams. 3. Sew strip along each top edge and sew on zipper. 4. Sew tab. 5. With right sides facing, sew side and bottom seams catching tab in place. 6. Open seams of side and bottom. Match seams and stitch each corner. 7. Cut front and back from fabric for lining and make inner case. Insert inner case into outer case with wrong sides facing. Turn in top edge of lining and slip-stitch to fabric for zipper. 8. Overcast a few stitches to secure at each side.

See photo for colors of Cosmetic Case shown at bottom

※ Add 0.7cm (¼″) for seam allowance unless otherwise indicated.

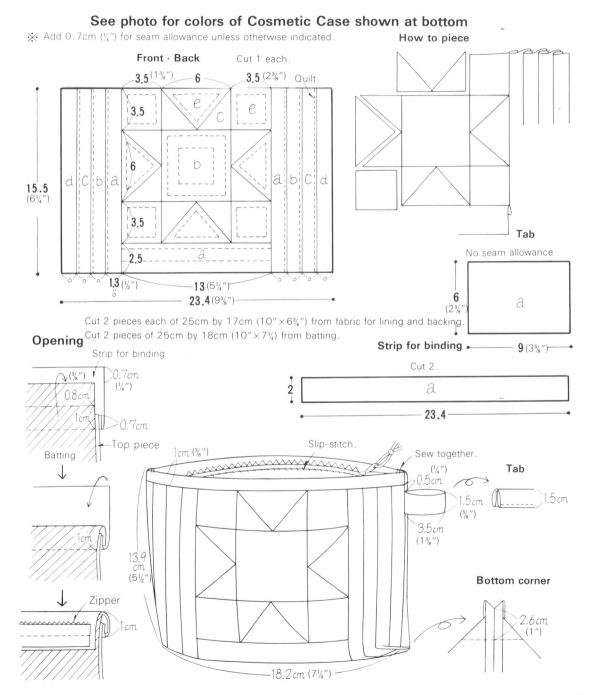

Instructions for Placemats on page 55 and for Bag on page 54.

Yo-Yo Flowers

Placemats
and Lunch Bag

Instructions on page 69.

Small Bag

X'mas Tree

Lunch Bag, *shown on page 52.*

MATERIALS: Floral print for top, 90cm by 30cm (36″ × 12″). Fabric for lining, 70cm by 20cm (28″×8″). Fabric for patches, yo-yos and strip. Backing and batting, 70cm by 30cm (28″×12″)each. **FINISHED SIZE:** See diagram. **DIRECTIONS:** 1. Join squares and appliqué onto top piece. (Leave two sides of last square un-stitched.) 2. Pin and baste top, batting and backing together.

Quilt diagonally in two directions. 3. Fold quilted piece in half with right sides facing and sew side seam. Turn to right side. Appliqué two sides of last square overlapping. 4. Make yo-yos and sew in place. 5. Sew casing in slip -stitch. 6. Pin and baste top, batting and backing of bottom and quilt. 7. With right sides facing, sew bottom and side together. 8. Make inner bag in same manner. 9. Insert inner bag into outer bag with wrong sides facing. Turn in seam allowance and slip-stitch inner bag onto outer bag. 10. Sew strap and insert into casing.

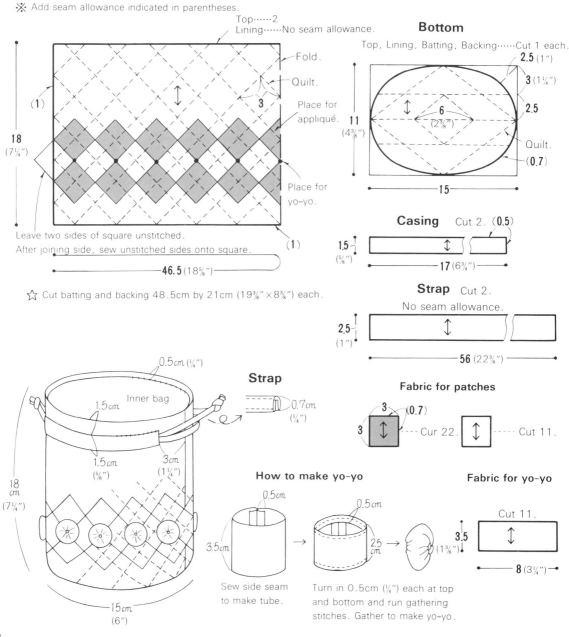

※ Add seam allowance indicated in parentheses.

Top……2
Lining……No seam allowance.

Fold.
Quilt.
Place for appliqué.
Place for yo-yo.
Leave two sides of square unstitched.
After joining side, sew unstitched sides onto square.

18 (7¼″)
3
(1)
(1)
46.5 (18⅝″)

☆ Cut batting and backing 48.5cm by 21cm (19⅜″×8⅜″) each.

Bottom

Top, Lining, Batting, Backing……Cut 1 each.

2.5 (1″)
3 (1¼″)
2.5
Quilt.
(0.7)
11 (4¾″)
6 (2⅜″)
15

Casing Cut 2. (0.5)

1.5 (⅝″)
17 (6¾″)

Strap Cut 2.
No seam allowance.

2.5 (1″)
56 (22⅜″)

Inner bag
0.5cm (¼″)
1.5cm
1.5cm
3cm (1¼″)
18 cm (7¼″)
15cm (6″)

Strap
0.7cm (¼″)

Fabric for patches

3
3
(0.7)
Cut 22.
Cut 11.

How to make yo-yo

0.5cm
0.5cm
3.5cm
2.5 cm
(1⅜″)

Sew side seam to make tube.

Turn in 0.5cm (¼″) each at top and bottom and run gathering stitches. Gather to make yo-yo.

Fabric for yo-yo

Cut 11.
3.5
8 (3¼″)

Placemats, *shown on page 52.*

MATERIALS: (FOR ONE): Floral print for top, fabric for backing and batting, 36cm by 28cm (14⅜″ × 11¼″) each. Fabric for lining, 37cm by 29cm (14¾″×11⅝″). Fabric for binding, 50cm (20″) square. Six-strand embroidery floss, No. 25 in olive green. For Placemat at top: Scraps of 7 different prints. Fabric for yo-yos. For Placemat at bottom: Scraps in dark and light olive green shades for patches; scraps of 3 different prints for yo-yos. Satin ribbon, 0.5cm by 17cm (¼″×6¾″). **FINISHED SIZE:** 28cm by 36cm (11¼″×14⅜″). **DIRECTIONS:** 1. Pin and baste top, batting and backing together and quilt. 2. Join patch pieces and make yo-yos. Appliqué in place. 3. Bind raw edges with bias-cut strip. 4. Slip-stitch lining onto back of quilted piece.

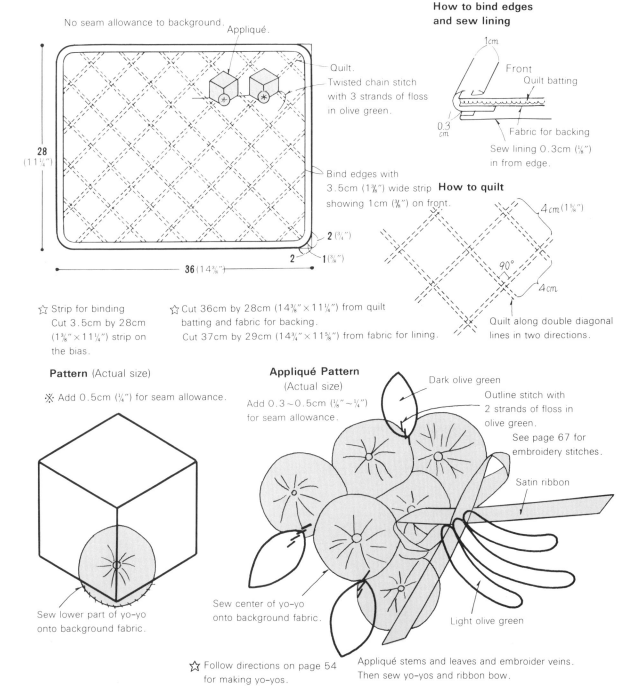

No seam allowance to background. Appliqué.

Quilt.
Twisted chain stitch with 3 strands of floss in olive green.

28 (11¼″)

Bind edges with 3.5cm (1⅜″) wide strip showing 1cm (⅜″) on front.

2 (¾″)

2 1 (¾″)

36 (14⅜″)

How to bind edges and sew lining

1cm
Front
Quilt batting
0.3 cm
Fabric for backing
Sew lining 0.3cm (⅛″) in from edge.

How to quilt

4cm (1⅝″)
90°
4cm
Quilt along double diagonal lines in two directions.

☆ Strip for binding Cut 3.5cm by 28cm (1⅜″×11¼″) strip on the bias.

☆ Cut 36cm by 28cm (14⅜″×11¼″) from quilt batting and fabric for backing. Cut 37cm by 29cm (14¾″×11⅝″) from fabric for lining.

Pattern (Actual size)

※ Add 0.5cm (¼″) for seam allowance.

Sew lower part of yo-yo onto background fabric.

Appliqué Pattern (Actual size)

Add 0.3~0.5cm (⅛″~¼″) for seam allowance.

Dark olive green

Outline stitch with 2 strands of floss in olive green.

See page 67 for embroidery stitches.

Satin ribbon

Sew center of yo-yo onto background fabric.

Light olive green

☆ Follow directions on page 54 for making yo-yos.

Appliqué stems and leaves and embroider veins. Then sew yo-yos and ribbon bow.

Instructions on page 58.

Girl

Girl Tote Bag

Instructions on page 70.

Berry Tote Bag

Berry

Girl Tote Bag, *shown on page 56.*

※ Add 1cm (⅜″) for seam allowance to borders
and 0.7cm (¼″) to other pieces.

Front   Cut 1 each.

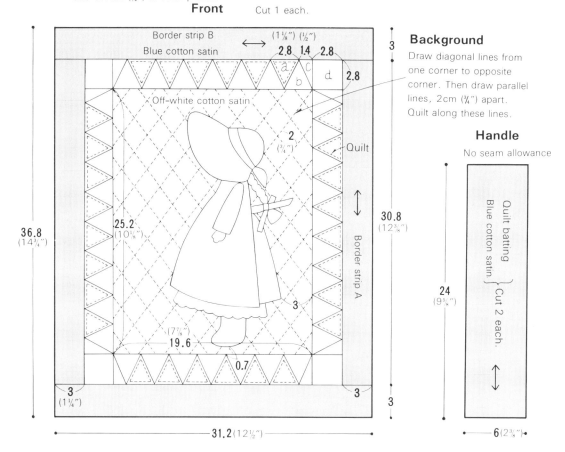

Border strip B
Blue cotton satin
(1⅛″) (½″)
2.8 1.4 2.8

Off-white cotton satin

a c
b d 2.8

3

Quilt

2
(¾″)

Border strip A

25.2
(10⅛″)

30.8
(12⅜″)

36.8
(14¾″)

3

(7⅞″)
19.6

0.7

3
(1¼″)

3

3

3

31.2 (12½″)

Background

Draw diagonal lines from
one corner to opposite
corner. Then draw parallel
lines, 2cm (¾″) apart.
Quilt along these lines.

Handle
No seam allowance

Quilt batting
Blue cotton satin } Cut 2 each.

24
(9⅝″)

6 (2⅜″)

☆ Blue cotton satin. Fabric for backing······Cut 1 each. } Cut 33.2cm by 38.8cm (13¼″×15½″)
Fabric for lining. Quilt batting······Cut 2each.

Opening
Handle

Outer
bag

Inner bag

Handle
Make handles covering rolled-up batting
with strip and slip-stitch.

2cm

Quilt Batting

8cm

33.8
cm
(13½″)

25.2cm
(10⅛″)

Outer
bag
Opening   Inner bag

4cm
(1⅝″)

Sew 4cm (1⅝″) each of outer
and inner bags individually.
Then, sew outer and inner bags
together at sides and bottom.

Detail for corner

3cm

Fold as shown and take
a few stitches at each corner.

Required number of pieces

a	Plain	Cut28.
b		32
c	Pattern	8
d		4

MATERIALS: Cotton fabric for patches: 80cm by 5cm (32″×2″) for (a); 90cm by 10cm (36″×4″) for (b), (c) and (d). Scraps of 4 different prints for appliqué. Blue cotton satin, 70cm by 40cm (28″×16″). Off-white cotton satin, 30cm (12″) square. Fabric for backing, 40cm (16″) square. Fabric for lining, 70cm by 40cm (28″×16″). Quilt batting, 80cm by 40cm (32″×16″). Scrap of gray felt. Cotton lace edging, 3cm by 18cm(1¼″×7¼″). Rose-pink satin ribbon, 0.5cm by 15cm (¼″×6″). Six-strand embroidery floss, No. 25 in light brown. **FINISHED SIZE:** See diagram. **DIRECTIONS:** 1. Appliqué girl onto off-white cotton satin. 2. Join pieces for inner border and sew onto appliquéd cotton satin. Then, sew on outer borders A and B. 3. Pin and baste top, batting and backing together. Quilt along quilting lines. 4. With right sides of quilted front and back facing, sew 4cm (1⅝″) of side seams from top edge. Sew inner bag in same manner. 5. Place outer and inner bags together and sew remaining sides and bottom. 6. Sew handles. 7. Turn to right side and turn in seam allowance at top edge. Sew ends of handles onto top edges. Slip-stitch folded edge of inner bag onto outer bag. 8. Take a few stitches at each corner.

Appliqué pattern (Actual size)

※ Add 0.7cm (¼″) for seam allowance except felt.

Tack band with thread and leave ends free.
Fray edge.
Make braid with 3 groups of 7 skeins each. Tack braid onto background.
Tie ribbon around end of braid.
Place lace edging under skirt.
Lace
No seam allowance
Felt

Instructions for **(A)** on page 62 and for **(B)** on page 72.

Tote Bags

B—*Dresden Plate* A—*Cathedral Window*

Instructions on page 74.

Tote Bag

Trip around the World

Cathedral Window Tote, *shown on page 60.*

MATERIALS: Light brown cotton fabric, 90cm by 200cm(36″×80″); 80cm by 5cm (32″×2″) for (a); 40cm by 5cm (16″×2″) each for (b) and (c); 45cm by 5cm (18″×2″) for (d); 20cm by 5cm (8″×2″) each for (e) and (f); 50cm by 5cm (20″×2″) for (g). Fabric for backing and for inner bag, 70cm by 50cm (28″×20″) each. Quilt batting, 110cm by 55cm (44″×22″). **FINISHED SIZE:** See diagram. **DIRECTIONS:** 1. Pin and baste light brown cotton, batting and backing together. Quilt single and double circles. 2. Make and join window patches.

Bind top edge of pocket. 3. Place joined piece on quilted fabric and stitch bottom of pocket onto background. Slip-stitch each side onto background fabric. 4. Fold in half with right sides facing, and sew side seams. Press seams open and stitch each corner. 5. Make inner bag. 6. Sew outer and inner bags together at each corner. 7. Bind top edge with strip and batting. 8. Make handles. Sew ends of handles onto wrong side of outer bag. 9. Turn in seam allowance of inner bag and slip-stitch.

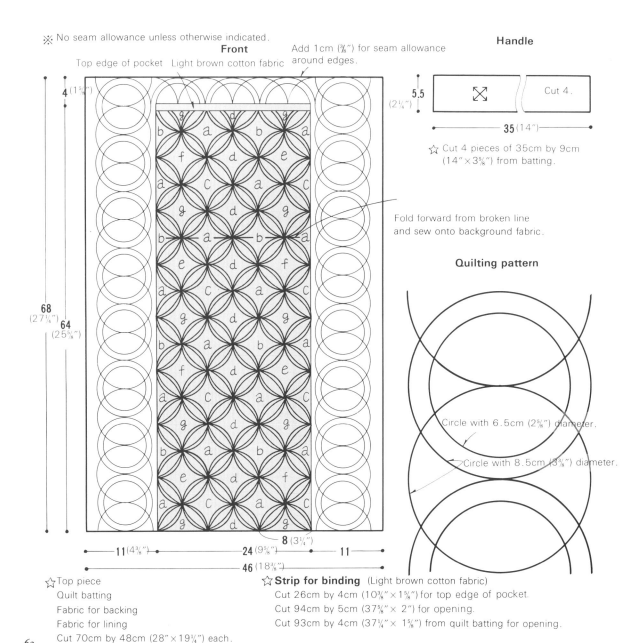

※ No seam allowance unless otherwise indicated.

Front

Top edge of pocket Light brown cotton fabric

Add 1cm (⅜″) for seam allowance around edges.

Handle

Cut 4.

5.5 (2¼″)

35 (14″)

☆ Cut 4 pieces of 35cm by 9cm (14″×3⅝″) from batting.

Fold forward from broken line and sew onto background fabric.

Quilting pattern

Circle with 6.5cm (2⅝″) diameter.

Circle with 8.5cm (3⅜″) diameter.

4 (1⅝″)

68 (27¼″)

64 (25⅝″)

8 (3¼″)

11 (4⅜″) 24 (9⅝″) 11

46 (18⅜″)

☆Top piece
Quilt batting
Fabric for backing
Fabric for lining
Cut 70cm by 48cm (28″×19¼″) each.

☆**Strip for binding** (Light brown cotton fabric)
Cut 26cm by 4cm (10⅜″×1⅝″) for top edge of pocket.
Cut 94cm by 5cm (37⅝″× 2″) for opening.
Cut 93cm by 4cm (37¼″× 1⅝″) from quilt batting for opening.

Cathedral window patchwork

How to make cathedral window patches

Background

Light brown cotton fabric
※ Add 1cm (⅜") for seam allowance.

16.8
(6¾")

Cut 24.

16.8

1. With right sides facing, fold base in half and sew side seams.

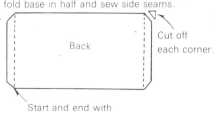

Back

Cut off each corner.

Start and end with a few backstitches.

2. Press seams open and fold as shown.

3. Sew to edge leaving 3cm (1¼) open. Turn to right side.

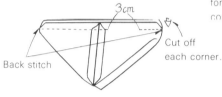

3cm

Cut off each corner.

Back stitch

4. Slip-stitch opening closed. Fold forward from broken line and sew corners at center catching all layers.

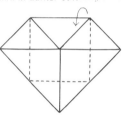

Fabric for window

No seam allowance

5
(2")

5

Required pieces of window patches

a	Cut 16.
b	8
c	8
d	9
e	4
f	4
g	10

5. Join required number of pieces by overcasting.

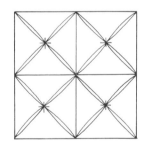

6. Center print square over seam. Fold edge in a curve over window patch and slip-stitch.

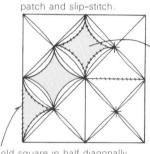

Take a few stitches to secure at beginning and ending.

Fold square in half diagonally and slip-stitch to bag catching base.

Opening

1cm (⅜")

3cm (1¼")

Quilt batting

Top piece

1.5cm (⅝")

Lining

Handle

2cm (¾")

Roll up batting and insert into handle.

Sew ends of handles securely.

11cm (4⅜")

Top edge of pocket

Bind edges with 4cm (1⁹⁄₁₆") strip showing 1cm (⅜") on front.

1cm

30.5 cm (12¼")

36cm (14⅜")

Detail for corner

5cm (2")

Inner bag

Outer bag

Sew corners of inner and outer bags together.

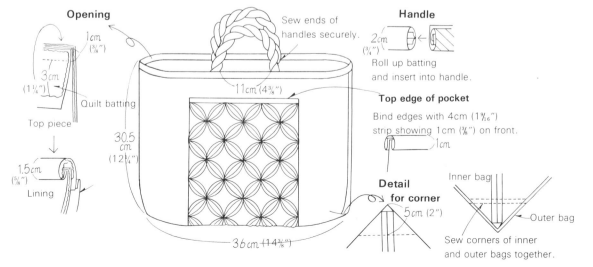

Stocking — F

Cathedral Window — AA'

Bell — C

Puff's Main Wreath — E

Christmas Ornaments

Candy Cane — B

Horse — D

Instructions for (A), (A') and (F) on page 77,
for (B), (D) and (E) on page 76
and for (C) on page 75.

Hints for Making Neat Patchwork

The following are some hints on making patchwork and quilts. Please read them carefully before you start.

Fabrics; One of the most important things in patchwork is choosing the most suitable colors and designs for your project. It is sometimes difficult to get the same kind of fabrics a book shows, but try to use your favorites, referring to the book and considering patterns and color cmbinations. Enjoy making your originals.

Color diagram:
Letters are used to indicate different colors or prints in this book. You could color the diagrams with colored pencils to get a clearer image of the design.

a	b	a
b	a	b
a	b	a

Make a sample for color placement: Cut a small piece of each fabric to be used and arrange them following a color placement plan. You may picture the finished piece in this way. Check carefully and change colors if necessary.

Color coordination: Consider the color of patches, main patterns, and background fabrics carefully. It is easy to coordinate solids and prints but it take more time to arrange a combination of prints. Arrange them considering large and small designs or dark and light shades, and you'll be able to make unique combinations of colors.

Make use of prints: Various kinds of prints are used in this book.
Prints with large pattern... Cut out designed area of prints and use them (see Bedspread on pages 16 & 17 and Mat on pages 20 & 21).
Border print... Make use of repeated patterns of border prints and quilt along designs (see Wall Hanging on page 13).

Make use of scraps: You may already have scraps of various kinds of fabrics stored from dress-making, patchwork or other needlecraft. Make as much use of them as possible, for each scrap may remind you of happy memories. Pillows on pages 32 & 33, Coasters on page 37 and Potholders on page 40 show good ways to use scraps.

Cutting: Use fabric from selvage to selvage for greatest economy. Cutting layout at right shows one example of placement of right-angled triangles. Notice that you don't have to add as much seam allowance. Place template on wrong side of fabric and mark shape with chalk or pencil. Cut two or three layers at one time for quick cutting.

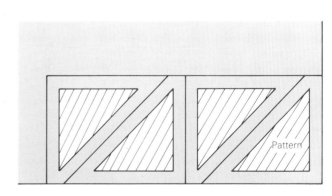

Pattern

Stitching and seams: Needless to say, all patches should be sewn in tiny, even stitches, but the following suggestion will help you to make neater patchwork. Pieces are stitched either from edge to edge or from mark to mark depending on the number of pieces meeting at one point. When you join squares, stitch from edge to edge and make one row of squares. Then join rows together. When you join diamonds to make a star, stitch from mark to mark so that seams are pressed open at center to avoid bulkiness. Seams are usually turned to one side, but they are sometimes turned to the side of the particular pattern to be shown. Always turn seams of lighter color to darker side.

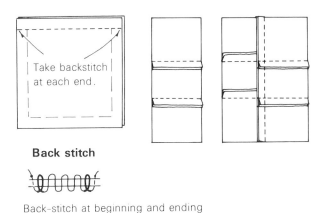

Back stitch

Back-stitch at beginning and ending of sewing with tiny stitches.

Turn seams to pattern.

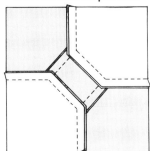

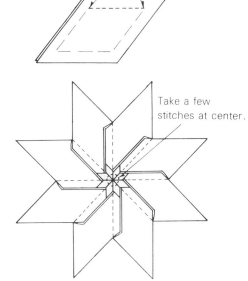

Turn seams to the same direction and open seams at center. Take a few stitches at center to avoid making a hole.

Batting: Use the most suitable material considering the size and purpose of the project.

Domett... This is tightly woven white cotton flannel, so backing fabric is not required when quilting.

Polyester quilt batting... This is light in weight and strong. It does not shrink when washed. When you make a large piece, use this for easy handling.

Flannel... Makes good interlining, for its brushed surface gives a soft effect to the work.

Helpful hints for quilting:

Transferring pattern: Trace quilting pattern onto tracing paper. Then transfer traced pattern onto fabric using dressmaker's carbon or washable ink. When drawing quilting lines or marking directly on the fabric, use a hard pencil.

Basting: Careful basting will make quilting neat and easy. Center top, batting and lining together. Baste at center first and work outward. Cut batting and lining larger than finished size and trim excess after quilting is finished.

How to baste

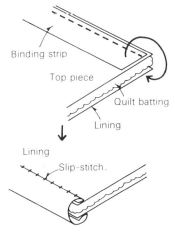

Quilting

After transferring pattern and basting are finished, quilt on quilting lines with even stitches.

Baste all the layers together radiating out from central point. Then baste along squares starting from inner one.

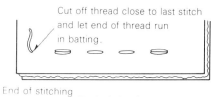

How to quilt

Cut off thread close to last stitch and let end of thread run in batting.

End of stitching

Backstitch twice.

Pull thread and let the knot sink inside.

How to finish raw edges

Place quilted piece flat and straighten all edges. Then finish raw edges with one of the following methods.

Binding

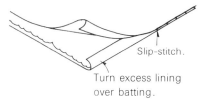

Binding strip

Top piece

Quilt batting

Lining

Lining

Slip-stitch.

Turn excess lining over top and slip-stitch.

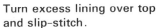

Slip-stitch.

Top piece

Lining

Turn in raw edges of top and lining and slip-stitch.

Slip-stitch.

Turn excess lining over batting.

How to join batting:

When joining two pieces of batting or lining together to make required size, join them at center for a neater finish. Place two pieces of batting side by side or thin out the area to be overlapped and overcast together.

Place side by side.

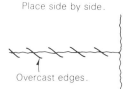

Overcast edges.

Overcast.

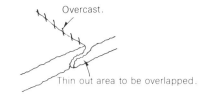

Thin out area to be overlapped.

Embroidery stitches used in the book

Running stitch

Work evenly spaced being careful not to pull thread too tight.

Outline stitch

2 in

out

French knot

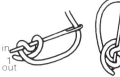

2 in
1 out

2

Back stitch

3 out
1 out
2 in

Straight stitch

1 out
2 in
3 out
4 in

Twisted chain stitch

4 in
5 out
3

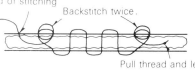

Mitten, *shown on page 40.*

MATERIALS: Plain quilted fabric, 50cm by 30cm (20″×12″). Scrap of print for appliqué. Brown print, 50cm (20″) square. **FINISHED SIZE:** See diagram. **DIRECTIONS:** 1. Appliqué triangle on back of mitten. Then appliqué pineapple. 2. With wrong sides facing, bind edges of gusset and top edge of palm side with 25cm (10″) long bias strip. 3. Bind bottom edges of back and palm individually with 16cm (6⅜″) long strip. With wrong sides facing, bind side edges of back and palm through top edge of back with 55cm (22″) long strip.

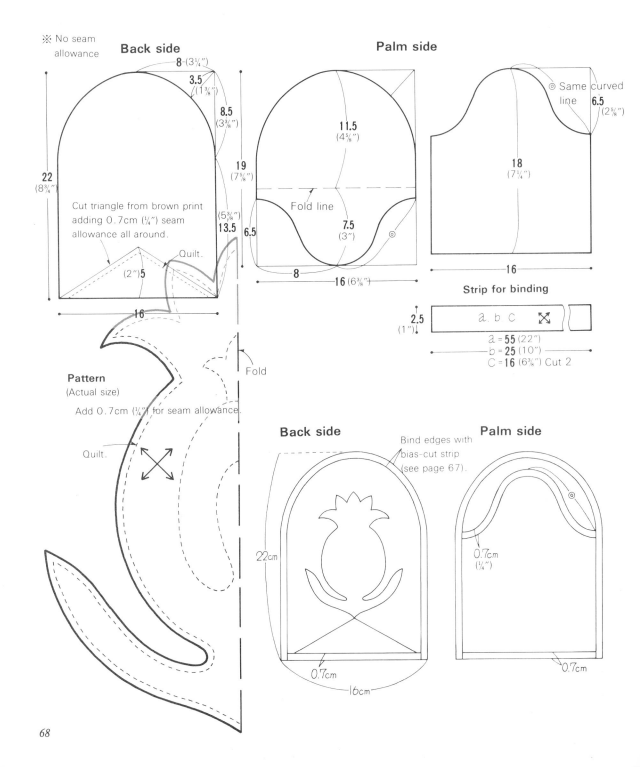

※ No seam allowance

Back side

8 (3¼″)
3.5 (1⅜″)
8.5 (3⅜″)
19 (7⅝″)
22 (8¾″)
(5⅜″) 13.5
6.5
16

Cut triangle from brown print adding 0.7cm (¼″) seam allowance all around.

Quilt.

(2″)5

Palm side

11.5 (4⅝″)
Fold line
7.5 (3″)
8
16 (6⅜″)

◎ Same curved line
6.5 (2⅝″)
18 (7¼″)
16

Strip for binding

2.5 (1″)

a. b. c

a = 55 (22″)
b = 25 (10″)
C = 16 (6⅜″) Cut 2

Pattern (Actual size)
Add 0.7cm (¼″) for seam allowance.

Quilt.

Fold

Back side

Bind edges with bias-cut strip (see page 67).

22cm
0.7cm
16cm

Palm side

0.7cm (¼″)
0.7cm

68

Small Bag, *shown on page 53.*

MATERIALS: Scraps of prints for appliqué. Scrap of white felt. Blue cotton fabric and backing fabric, 50cm by 30cm (20″×12″) each. Blue gray cotton fabric, 90cm by 40cm (36″×16″). Quilt batting, 90cm by 30cm (36″×12″). **FINISHED SIZE:** See diagram. **DIRECTIONS:** 1. Pin and baste top, batting and backing together. Quilt diagonally in two directions. 2. Join pieces for tree and appliqué in place. Appliqué snow (see photo). 3. Place front and back of top with right sides facing. Place front and back of lining in same manner on top pieces. Sew side and bottom, seams of 4 layers together. 4. Sew handles. 5. Turn to right side. Sew bias-cut strip onto top edge of bag catching ends of handles. 6. Turn inside out and take a few stitches at each corner.

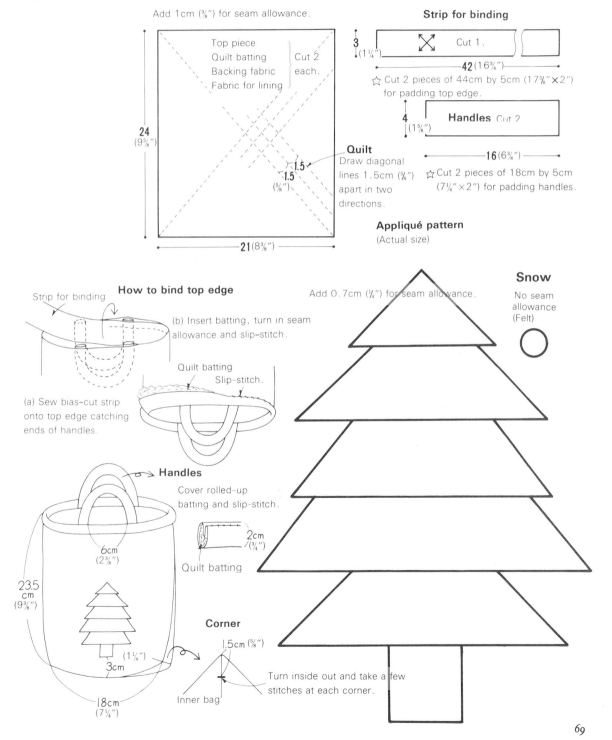

Add 1cm (⅜″) for seam allowance.

Top piece
Quilt batting
Backing fabric
Fabric for lining

Cut 2 each.

24 (9⅝″)

21 (8⅜″)

1.5
1.5 (⅝″)

Quilt
Draw diagonal lines 1.5cm (⅝″) apart in two directions.

Strip for binding

3 (1¼″)

Cut 1.

42 (16¾″)

☆ Cut 2 pieces of 44cm by 5cm (17⅞″×2″) for padding top edge.

4 (1⅝″)

Handles Cut 2

16 (6¾″)

☆ Cut 2 pieces of 18cm by 5cm (7¼″×2″) for padding handles.

Appliqué pattern
(Actual size)

How to bind top edge

Strip for binding

(b) Insert batting, turn in seam allowance and slip-stitch.

Quilt batting
Slip-stitch.

(a) Sew bias-cut strip onto top edge catching ends of handles.

Handles
Cover rolled-up batting and slip-stitch.

2cm (¾″)

Quilt batting

23.5 cm (9⅜″)

6cm (2⅜″)

(1¼″)

3cm

18cm (7¼″)

Corner

1.5cm (⅝″)

Inner bag

Turn inside out and take a few stitches at each corner.

Add 0.7cm (¼″) for seam allowance.

Snow
No seam allowance (Felt)

Tote Bag, *shown on page 57.*

MATERIALS: Beige cotton fabric, 22cm by 46cm (8¾″×18⅜″). Checked fabric, 68cm by 92cm (27¼″×36¾″). Flannel and fabric for lining, 56cm by 92cm (22⅜″×36¾″) each. Coarse fabric for backing, 22cm by 46cm (8¾″×18⅜″). Quilt batting, 94cm by 6cm (37⅝″×2⅜″). Baby yarn. Sewing thread, #30 in light brown. Polyester fiberfill. **FINISHED SIZE:** See diagram. **DIRECTIONS:** 1. Place beige fabric on backing and quilt along quilting lines. Join quilted piece with checked fabric. 2. With right sides facing, sew 5cm (2″) of side seams of front and back together with flannel. Sew front and back of lining in same manner. 3. Place top and lining together and sew remaining side and bottom seams. 4. Sew handles and strap. 5. Turn to right side. Turn in seam allowances of top and lining, sew ends of handles securely and slip-stitch lining to top. 6. Fold each corner as shown and sew to side seams.

Quilting pattern
(Actual size)

※ 1 strand of floss in sewing thread, #30 in light brown.

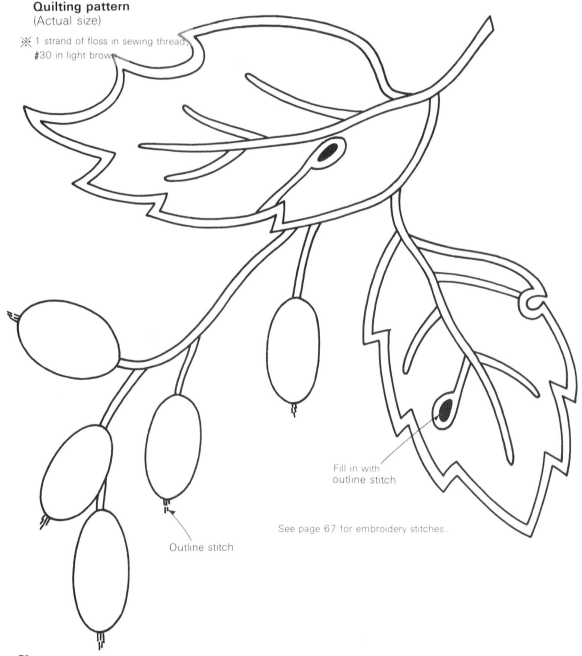

Fill in with outline stitch

Outline stitch

See page 67 for embroidery stitches.

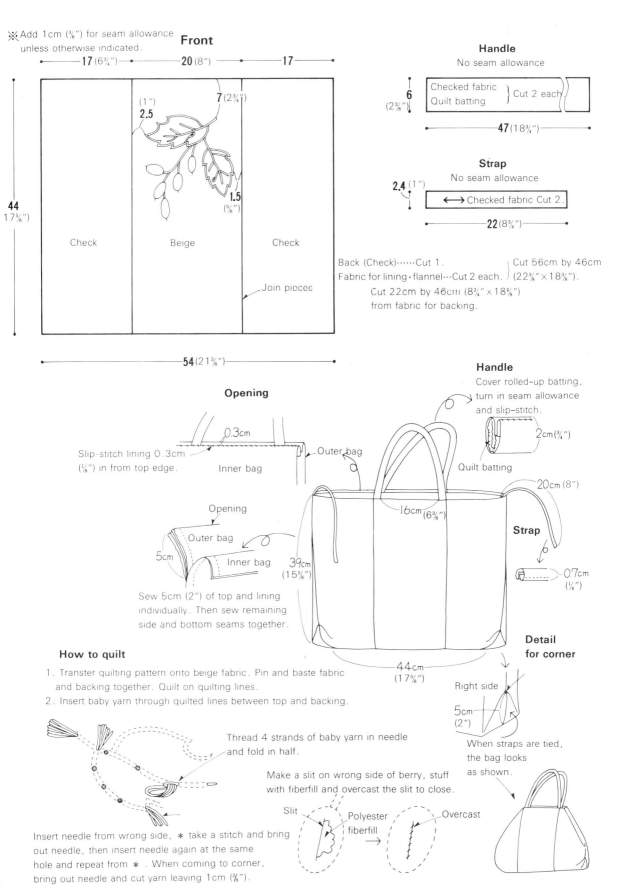

※ Add 1cm (⅜″) for seam allowance unless otherwise indicated.

Front

17 (6¾″) — 20 (8″) — 17

44
(17⅝″)

2.5 (1″)
7 (2¾″)
1.5 (⅝″)

Check   Beige   Check

Join pieces

54 (21⅝″)

Handle
No seam allowance

Checked fabric } Cut 2 each.
Quilt batting

6 (2⅜″)

47 (18¾″)

Strap
No seam allowance

2.4 (1″)

← Checked fabric Cut 2. →

22 (8¾″)

Back (Check)······Cut 1.
Fabric for lining·flannel···Cut 2 each. } Cut 56cm by 46cm (22⅜″ × 18⅜″).
Cut 22cm by 46cm (8¾″ × 18⅜″) from fabric for backing.

Opening

Slip-stitch lining 0.3cm (⅛″) in from top edge.

0.3cm
Outer bag
Inner bag

Opening
Outer bag
5cm
Inner bag

Sew 5cm (2″) of top and lining individually. Then sew remaining side and bottom seams together.

Handle
Cover rolled-up batting, turn in seam allowance and slip-stitch.

2cm (¾″)
Quilt batting

16cm (6⅜″)
39cm (15⅝″)
44cm (17⅝″)

20cm (8″)

Strap

0.7cm (¼″)

Detail for corner

Right side

5cm (2″)

When straps are tied, the bag looks as shown.

How to quilt

1. Transfer quilting pattern onto beige fabric. Pin and baste fabric and backing together. Quilt on quilting lines.
2. Insert baby yarn through quilted lines between top and backing.

Thread 4 strands of baby yarn in needle and fold in half.

Insert needle from wrong side, ＊ take a stitch and bring out needle, then insert needle again at the same hole and repeat from ＊. When coming to corner, bring out needle and cut yarn leaving 1cm (⅜″).

Make a slit on wrong side of berry, stuff with fiberfill and overcast the slit to close.

Slit
Polyester fiberfill
Overcast

Dresden Plate Tote, *shown on page 60.*

MATERIALS: Cotton fabric: 19cm by 10cm (7⅝″ × 4″) for (a); 10cm (4″) square each for (b) − (h); olive green, 35cm by 15cm (14″ × 6″). Unbleached sheeting, 90cm by 100cm (36″ × 40″). Fabrics for backing and inner bag, 90cm by 85cm (36″ × 34″) each. Quilt batting, 120cm by 70cm (48″ × 28″). 46cm (18⅜″) long zipper. **FINISHED SIZE:** See diagram. **DIRECTIONS:** 1. Join patch pieces and appliqué on front. 2. Pin and baste front, batting and backing together. Quilt. 3. Pin and baste back, batting and backing together. Quilt along plate pattern and diagonal lines (see quilting pattern). 4. Sew darts of front and back individually. Sew darts of inner bag. Trim excess fabric at bottom. 5. With right sides facing, sew front and back together. 6. Turn to right side. Sew strip along top edge and sew zipper in place. 7. Sew inner bag and insert into outer bag. Turn in seam allowance of top edge and slip-stitch onto fabric for zipper. 8. Make six padded straps, divide into two groups and braid. Finish end of braid with small piece of fabric. Attach ends of braids in place.

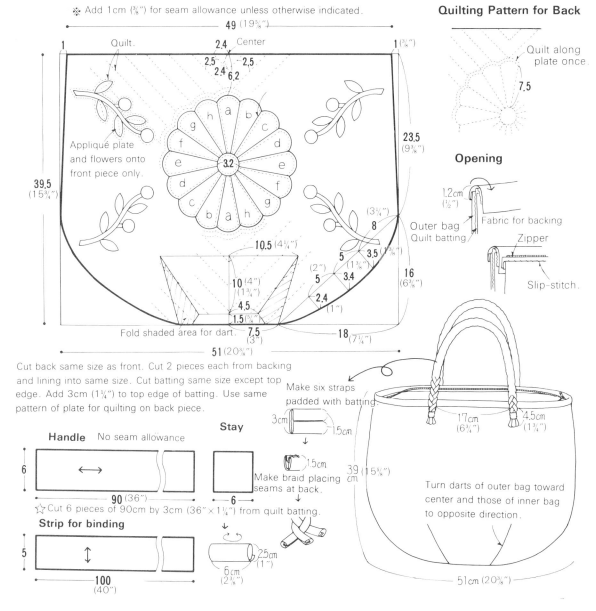

Bud Cut 2 pieces each reversing pattern.

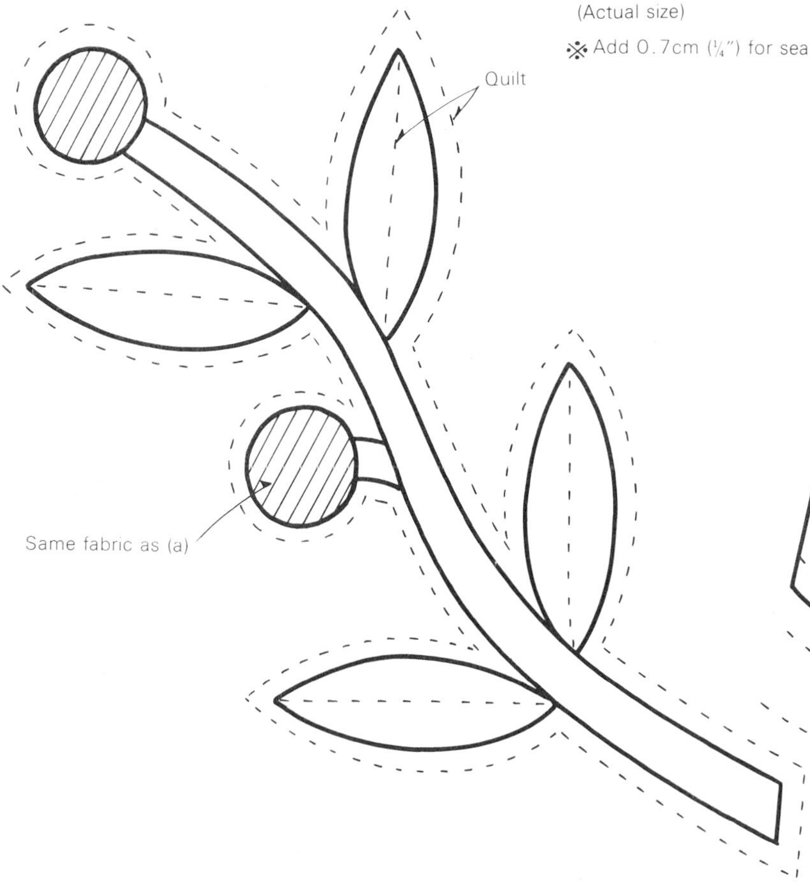

Quilt
Same fabric as (a)

Appliqué patterns
(Actual size)
※ Add 0.7cm (¼") for seam allowance.

Plate pattern

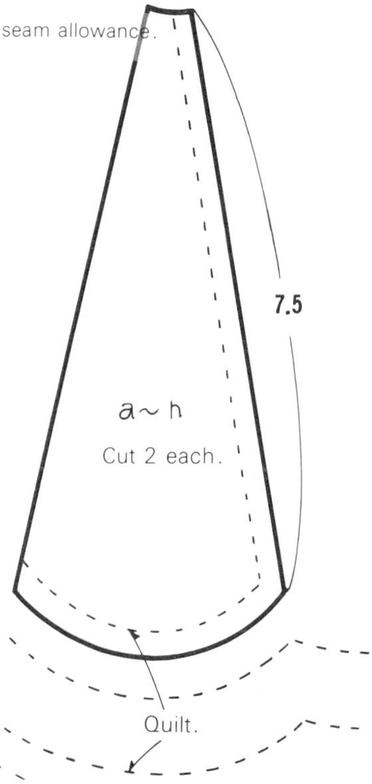

7.5
a~h
Cut 2 each.
Quilt.

Continued from page 47.

Appliqué patterns
(Actual size)
※ Add 0.5cm (¼") for seam allowance.

Flower & Center

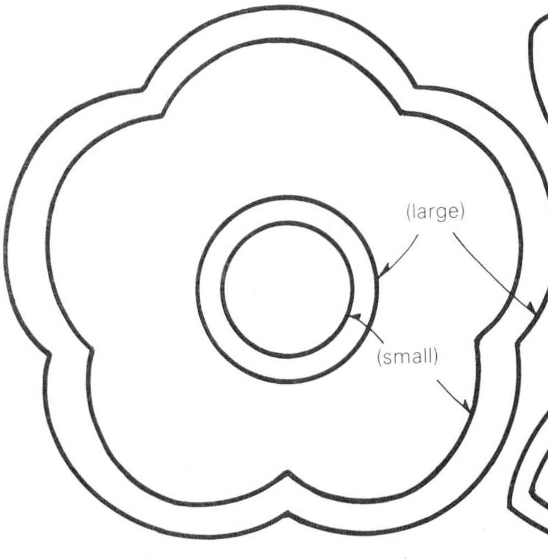

(large)
(small)

Bud

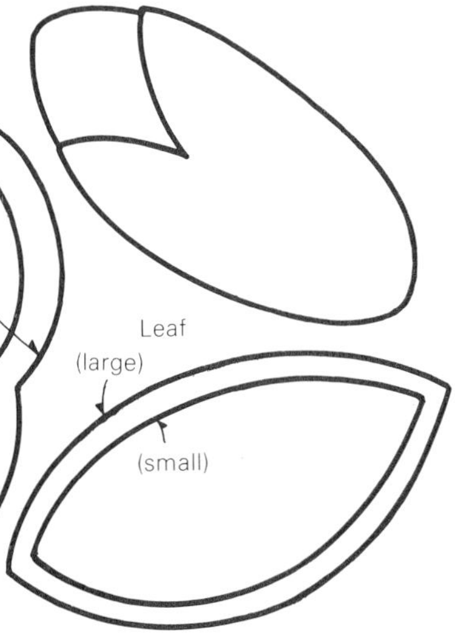

Leaf
(large)
(small)

Required number of pieces

Flower (large)	Pink	Cut 1.
	Red	1
Center (large)	2	
Flower (small)	Pink	1
	Red	1
Center (small)	2	
But	Red	2
	Check	2
Leaf (large)	3	
Leaf (small)	Check	2
	Print	3

Trip Around the World Tote, *shown on page 61.*

MATERIALS: Cotton fabric: 90cm by 60cm (36″×24″) each for (a) and (b); 90cm by 12cm (36″×4¾″) for (c); 90cm by 18cm (36″×7¼″) for (d); 90cm by 50cm (36″×20″) for (e). Flannel, 90cm (36″) square. Six-strand embroidery floss, No, 25 in light blue. **FINISHED SIZE:** See diagram. **DIRECTIONS:** 1. Join pieces carefully referring to photo for placement of colors. Join ◎—marked sides together to make tube. 2. Insert flannel into tube and quilt along seams of each square. 3. With right sides facing, fold fabric for inner bag in half, place flannel and sew side seams.

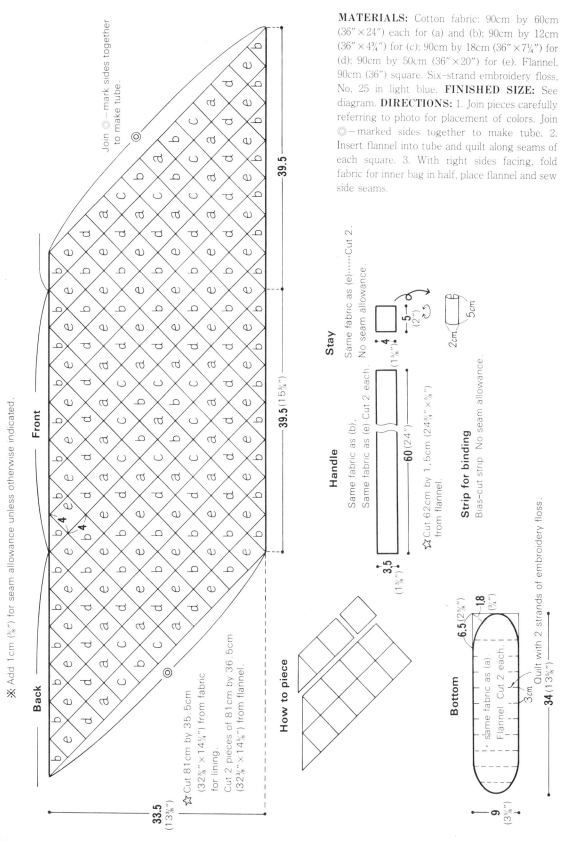

※ Add 1cm (⅜″) for seam allowance unless otherwise indicated.

Join ◎ — mark sides together to make tube.

Back **Front**

39.5

39.5 (15¾″)

☆ Cut 81cm by 35.5cm (32⅜″×14¼″) from fabric for lining.
Cut 2 pieces of 81cm by 36.5cm (32⅜″×14⅝″) from flannel.

How to piece

33.5 (13⅜″)

Stay

Same fabric as (e)......Cut 2
No seam allowance.

4 (1⅝″)

5 (2″)

2cm   5cm

Handle

Same fabric as (b).
Same fabric as (e) Cut 2 each.

60 (24″)

3.5 (1⅜″)

☆ Cut 62cm by 1.5cm (24¾″×⅝″) from flannel.

Strip for binding

Bias-cut strip No seam allowance.

Bottom

6.5 (2⅝″)   .18 (¾″)

3cm

34 (13⅜″)

same fabric as (a).
Flannel Cut 2 each.

Quilt with 2 strands of embroidery floss.

9 (3⅝″)

74

4. Sandwich 2 pieces of flannel with bottom pieces of outer bag and quilt. 5. Insert inner bag into outer bag. Place bottom with wrong sides facing and bind edges together. 6. Fold excess flannel and bind top edge with strip. 7. Sew 4 straps and insert rolled-up flannel into each strap. 8. Twist two straps together and attach in place.

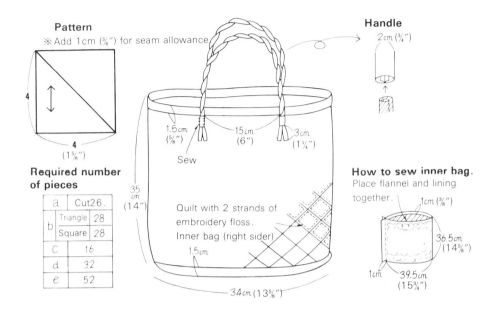

Pattern

※ Add 1cm (⅜″) for seam allowance.

4

4
(1⅝″)

Required number of pieces

a	Cut26.	
b	Triangle	28
	Square	28
c	16	
d	32	
e	52	

Handle

2cm (¾″)

1.5cm (⅝″)   15cm (6″)   3cm (1¼″)

Sew

35cm (14″)

Quilt with 2 strands of embroidery floss.
Inner bag (right sider)

1.5cm

34cm (13⅝″)

How to sew inner bag.
Place flannel and lining together.

1cm (⅜″)

36.5cm (14⅝″)

1cm   39.5cm (15¾″)

Christmas Ornaments, *shown on page 64.*

For Bell: MATERIALS: Scraps of two different prints. Fabric for lining, 24cm by 11cm (9⅝″×4⅜″). Polyester fiberfill. Ribbon. 2 bells. **FINISHED SIZE:** See pattern. **DIRECTIONS:** 1. Join 3 pieces each together for top. With right sides facing, sew top and lining together. Turn to right side. With right sides facing, sew side seams of top and lining leaving opening for turning. Turn to right side. 3. Insert lining into top, stuff with fiberfill and slip-stitch opening closed. Attach ribbon bow, bells and string for hanging.

Bell

Pattern
(Actual size)

Add 0.7cm (¼″) for seam allowance.

Top piece (a), (b), (c) ⎫ Cut 2 each.
Lining ⎭
(Cut one piece of bell shape.)

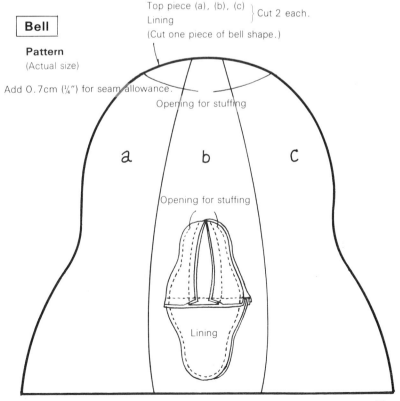

Opening for stuffing

a   b   c

Opening for stuffing

Lining

Patterns (Actual size)

Add 0.7cm (¼") for seam allowance unless otherwise indicated.

For Candy Cane: **MATERIALS:** Scraps of 2 different prints. Polyester fiberfill. Ribbon. Bell. **FINISHED SIZE:** See pattern. **DIRECTIONS:** With right sides facing, sew two pieces together leaving opening for turning. Turn to right side, stuff with fiberfill and slip-stitch opening closed. Make two canes. Assemble them as shown and attach ribbon bow, bell and string for hanging.

For Wreath: **MATERIALS:** Scraps of cotton fabric for (a), (b) and (c). Polyester fiberfill. Ribbon. Bell. **FINISHED SIZE:** See pattern. **DIRECTIONS:** 1. Make tuck at center of three sides of (a) and (b). Sew (a) and (c) or (b) and (c) together with right sides facing leaving bottom open. Turn to right side, stuff with fiberfill and slip-stitch opening closed. 2. Join puffs together placing (a) and (b) alternately. Attach ribbon bow, bell and string for hanging.

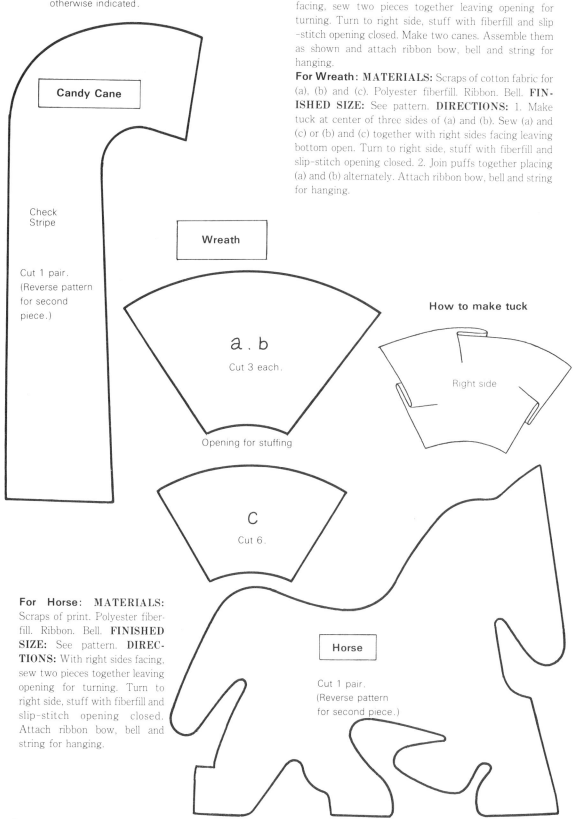

Candy Cane

Check Stripe

Cut 1 pair.
(Reverse pattern for second piece.)

Wreath

a . b

Cut 3 each.

Opening for stuffing

How to make tuck

Right side

C

Cut 6.

For Horse: **MATERIALS:** Scraps of print. Polyester fiberfill. Ribbon. Bell. **FINISHED SIZE:** See pattern. **DIRECTIONS:** With right sides facing, sew two pieces together leaving opening for turning. Turn to right side, stuff with fiberfill and slip-stitch opening closed. Attach ribbon bow, bell and string for hanging.

Horse

Cut 1 pair.
(Reverse pattern for second piece.)

For Stocking: MATERIALS: Scraps of 5 different prints. Fabric for lining. Quilt batting. Ribbon. Bell. **FINISHED SIZE:** See pattern: **DIRECTIONS:** 1. Pin and baste batting and lining together. Place piece (a) on basted batting. Place piece (b) on (a) with right sides facing. Sew along seam line catching all layers. Join remaining pieces in same manner. 2. With right sides facing, sew front and back together. Turn to right side. Turn in seam allowance at top edge and slip-stitch. Attach ribbon bow, bell and string for hanging.

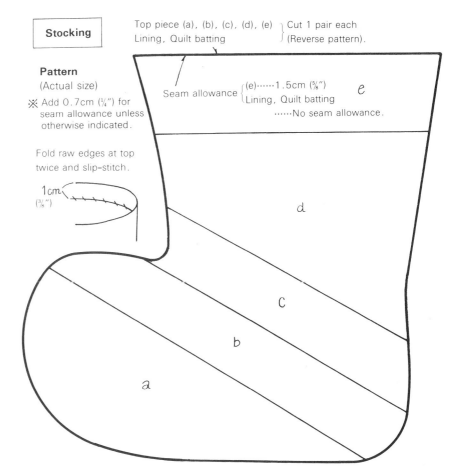

| Stocking |

Top piece (a), (b), (c), (d), (e) ⎫ Cut 1 pair each
Lining, Quilt batting ⎬ (Reverse pattern).

Pattern
(Actual size)

※ Add 0.7cm (¼") for seam allowance unless otherwise indicated.

Seam allowance { (e)······1.5cm (⅝")
Lining, Quilt batting ······No seam allowance.

Fold raw edges at top twice and slip-stitch.

1cm (⅜")

For Cathedral Window Ornament: MATERIALS: (FOR ONE): Plain cotton fabric, 36cm by 18cm (14⅜" × 7¼"). Print, 9cm by 4.5cm (3⅝" × 1¾"). Polyester fiberfill. **DIRECTIONS:** Make as shown below referring to page 62.

| Cathedral window |

Background

※ Add 1cm (⅜") for seam allowance.

16 (6⅜")

16

Fabric for window

No seam allowance

4.5 (1¾") | Cut 2 | 4.5

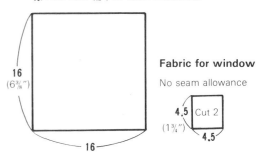

With wrong sides facing, overcast two pieces together. Fold as shown.

Place square piece on seam, fold edges as shown and slip-stitch.

Make back in same manner.

Overcast bottom edges together stuff with fiberfill and overcast top edges. Attach string for hanging.

Slip-stitch

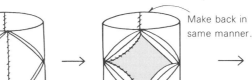

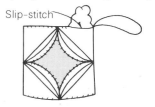

Continued from page 3.

Quilting Pattern for B (Actual size)

Quilting lines for background

Center